Global Health Governance

In light of scares about potential pandemics such as swine and avian flu, the issue of global health and its governance is of increasing concern to scholars and practitioners of medicine, public health, social work, and international politics alike.

Providing a concise and informative introduction to how global health is governed, this book:

- explores the various ways in which we understand global health governance;
- explains the "nuts and bolts" of the traditional institutions of global health governance, highlights key frameworks and treaties and their relative successes and failings;
- examines the actors in global health governance, their purpose, influence and impact; and
- offers an in depth analysis of the effectiveness of global health interventions, focusing particularly on HIV/AIDS, tuberculosis and malaria.

Highlighting the wide variety of actors, issues and approaches involved, this work shows the complex nature of global health governance, encouraging the reader to examine who or what really governs global health, to what outcome, and for whom.

Sophie Harman is a Senior Lecturer in the Department of International Politics, City University, London.

Routledge Global Institutions Series

Edited by Thomas G. Weiss
The CUNY Graduate Center, New York, USA
and Rorden Wilkinson
University of Manchester, UK

About the series

The Global Institutions Series is designed to provide readers with comprehensive, accessible, and informative guides to the history, structure, and activities of key international organizations as well as books that deal with topics of key importance in contemporary global governance. Every volume stands on its own as a thorough and insightful treatment of a particular topic, but the series as a whole contributes to a coherent and complementary portrait of the phenomenon of global institutions at the dawn of the millennium.

Books are written by recognized experts, conform to a similar structure, and cover a range of themes and debates common to the series. These areas of shared concern include the general purpose and rationale for organizations, developments over time, membership, structure, decision-making procedures, and key functions. Moreover, current debates are placed in historical perspective alongside informed analysis and critique. Each book also contains an annotated bibliography and guide to electronic information as well as any annexes appropriate to the subject matter at hand.

The volumes currently published are:

60 Global Health Governance (2012)
by Sophie Harman (City University, London)

59 The Council of Europe (2012)
by Martyn Bond (University of London)

58 The Security Governance of Regional Organizations (2011)
edited by Emil J. Kirchner (University of Essex) and Roberto Domínguez (Suffolk University)

57 The United Nations Development Programme and System (2011)
by Stephen Browne (FUNDS Project)

56 The South Asian Association for Regional Cooperation (2011)
An emerging collaboration architecture
by Lawrence Sáez (University of London)

Private Foundations and Development Partnerships
by Michael Moran (Swinburne University of Technology)

The Changing Political Map of Global Governance
by Anthony Payne (University of Sheffield) and Stephen Robert Buzdugan (Manchester Metropolitan University)

Decolonization, Sovereignty, and the African Union
by Martin Welz (University of Konstanz)

Feminist Strategies in International Governance
edited by Gülay Caglar (Humboldt University of Berlin), Elisabeth Prügl (Graduate Institute of International and Development Studies, Geneva), Susanne Zwingel (SUNY Potsdam)

Private Foundations and Development Partnerships
by Michael Moran (Swinburne University of Technology)

For further information regarding the series, please contact:

Craig Fowlie, Senior Publisher, Politics & International Studies
Taylor & Francis
2 Park Square, Milton Park, Abingdon
Oxford OX14 4RN, UK
+44 (0)207 842 2057 Tel
+44 (0)207 842 2302 Fax
Craig.Fowlie@tandf.co.uk
www.routledge.com

Global Health Governance

Sophie Harman

Routledge
Taylor & Francis Group

LONDON AND NEW YORK

First published 2012 by Routledge
2 Park Square, Milton Park, Abingdon, Oxon, OX14 4RN

Simultaneously published in the USA and Canada
by Routledge
711 Third Avenue, New York, NY 10017

Routledge is an imprint of the Taylor & Francis Group, an informa business

British Library Cataloguing in Publication Data
A catalogue record for this book is available from the British Library

Library of Congress Cataloging in Publication Data
Harman, Sophie.
  Global health governance / Sophie Harman.
    p. ; cm. – (Routledge global institutions series ; 60)
  Includes bibliographical references and index.
  1. World health. 2. Medical policy. 3. Medical laws and legislation,
International. I. Title. II. Series: Global institutions series ; 60.
  [DNLM: 1. World Health. 2. Health Policy–economics. 3. International
Cooperation. 4. Politics. 5. Socioeconomic Factors. WA 530.1]
  RA441.H37 2011
  362.1–dc23
            2011020542

ISBN 13: 978-0-415-56157-0 (hbk)
ISBN 13: 978-0-415-56158-7 (pbk)
ISBN 13: 978-0-203-15781-7 (ebk)

Typeset in Times New Roman
by Taylor & Francis Books

Printed and bound in Great Britain by
TJ International Ltd, Padstow, Cornwall

Contents

Illustrations

Figures

Box

Foreword

The current volume is the sixtieth title in a dynamic series on global institutions. These books provide readers with definitive guides to the most visible aspects of what many of us know as "global governance." Remarkable as it may seem, there exist relatively few books that offer in-depth treatments of prominent global bodies, processes, and associated issues, much less an entire series of concise and complementary volumes. Those that do exist are either out of date, inaccessible to the non-specialist reader, or seek to develop a specialized understanding of particular aspects of an institution or process rather than offer an overall account of its functioning and situate it within the increasingly dense global institutional network. Similarly, existing books have often been written in highly technical language or have been crafted "in-house" and are notoriously self-serving and narrow.

The advent of electronic media has undoubtedly helped research and teaching by making data and primary documents of international organizations more widely available, but it has complicated matters as well. The growing reliance on the Internet and other electronic methods of finding information about key international organizations and processes has served, ironically, to limit the educational and analytical materials to which most readers have ready access—namely, books. Public relations documents, raw data, and loosely refereed websites do not make for intelligent analysis. Official publications compete with a vast amount of electronically available information, much of which is suspect because of its ideological or self-promoting slant. Paradoxically, a growing range of purportedly independent websites offering analyses of the activities of particular organizations has emerged, but one inadvertent consequence has been to frustrate access to basic, authoritative, readable, critical, and well-researched texts. The market for such has actually been reduced by the ready availability of varying quality electronic materials.

For those of us who teach, research, and operate in the area, such restricted access to information and analyses has been frustrating. We were delighted when Routledge saw the value of a series that bucks this trend and provides key reference points to the most significant global institutions and issues. They are betting that serious students and professionals will want serious analyses. We have assembled a first-rate team of authors to address that market. Our intention is to provide one-stop shopping for all readers—students (both undergraduate and postgraduate), negotiators, diplomats, practitioners from non-governmental and intergovernmental organizations, and interested parties alike—seeking insights into the most prominent institutional aspects of global governance.

Global Health Governance

The inclusion of a book on global health governance in this series on global institutions is of course something of a "no-brainer." HIV/AIDS, SARS, and the Avian influenza have drawn attention to the necessity for cooperation across borders. But these more recent pandemics merely emphasize an older reality. The continued prevalence of a host of treatable and untreatable infectious diseases, the persistence (and all-too-often the growth) of damaging working environments, poor and restricted access to adequate sanitation and clean drinking water, under-nourishment, poor maternal healthcare, lack of access to (and often restrictions in the distribution of) vital medicines, pollution, and poor hygiene, among many others, have combined to ensure that health is a major focus on the work of many global institutions. These range not just from those that one would expect to deal with health issues, such as the World Health Organization and the Food and Agriculture Organization, but also those that might at first seem a little peripheral to the issue but which actually play an important role, such as the World Trade Organization and the International Monetary Fund.[1] These topics and institutions, in fact, are prominent features in other volumes in this series.[2]

There are, moreover, scholarly reasons for including this book in the series. Dealing with the cross-border effects of health and ill-health is not only a contemporary challenge of global governance but also has been a core concern of international organization as a process since it began with gusto in the mid-nineteenth century. Then, as another contributor to this series Craig Murphy writes, health and securing improvements therein was intrinsically bound up with the spread and acceleration of another, equally as entwined process, industrialization.[3]

Today, the governance of health and the global economy remain inexorably entwined, though not always for the best of reasons. This first-rate analysis explains, among many other things, why.

Few people are as well qualified to write this book as Sophie Harman. Sophie is Senior Lecturer at City University, London, and a graduate of the University of Manchester who has studied global health throughout her professional career. She is not just a student of global health but a practitioner as well. Widely consulted by UN institutions and a co-founder of a key nongovernmental organization (Trans Tanz)[4] in the fight against global poverty and ill-health, Sophie's encyclopedic knowledge and insights are much in evidence in the pages that follow. A more definitive guide to global health governance we could not have asked for. It is the perfect complement to our other volumes on health and related issues.

We thoroughly recommend this book to scholars, practitioners, and students of international relations, international organization and global governance. As always, we welcome comments and suggestions from our readers.

Thomas G. Weiss, The CUNY Graduate Center, New York, USA
Rorden Wilkinson, University of Manchester, UK
June 2011

Acknowledgments

Thank you to Rorden Wilkinson and Thomas Weiss for asking me to write this book. I am flattered that they thought me competent to deliver on such a task. I would like to thank everyone who participated in the research and gave up their time to talk to me and the staff at the WHO archives; every care has been taken not to misrepresent them. Special thanks to the Department of International Politics at City University for sponsoring my research in Geneva and the staff at the British Library. I am excited to be part of a growing field of scholarship on global health governance. Much of my research builds on that of Kelley Lee, Adam Kamradt-Scott, Andrew Harmer, Colin McInnes, Simon Rushton, Owain Williams, Stefan Elbe, Jeremy Youde, Garrett Brown, and Frank Lisk—I look forward to discussing the book with them, and no doubt disagreeing on parts! Part of this growing field are the students that have taken my class on the Global Politics of Health and Disease at City; their input, interests, and participation have framed the content of this book.

All graphs and data used in this book were compiled by Alejandro Pena, currently a PhD candidate at City. He is a great research assistant and a useful addition to the book. All data analysis and presentation have been done by him; however, I take full responsibility for any errors or misrepresentation in how the data have been used.

Thanks to my Mum for her constant gripes about privatization in the NHS and my Dad who every day used to ask the teenage me what I had done to justify my existence: this seems to be a question that haunts institutions of global health. Thanks to my family and friends for support and fun, particularly Hannah Lloyd, northwest England's premier biomedical scientist for checking my use of health terminology and Kieran Read for backing everything I do with humor and confidence.

Sections of chapters 3 and 5 appear in Sophie Harman, *The World Bank and HIV/AIDS: Setting a Global Agenda* (Routledge, 2010), but have been significantly updated. Sections of chapters 3 and 6 appear in Adrian Kay and Owain D. Williams, eds., *Global Health Governance* (Palgrave Macmillan, 2009), reproduced with permission of the publisher.

Abbreviations

ACT	Artemsin combination therapy
AMC	Advanced Market Commitment
AIDS	Acquired immunodeficiency syndrome
BCG	Bacille Calmette Guerin
CCMs	Country coordinating mechanisms
CDC	Centers for Disease Control and Prevention
DDT	Dichloro-diphenyl-trichlorothane
DFID	Department for International Development (UK)
DOTS	Directly Observed Treatment, Short Term
ECOSOC	Economic and Social Council
FAO	Food and Agriculture Organization
FCTC	Framework Convention on Tobacco Control
FIND	Foundation for Innovative New Diagnostics
GATT	General Agreement on Tariffs and Trade
GAVI	Global Alliance for Vaccines and Immunisation
GPA	Global Program on HIV/AIDS
GRID	Gay related immune deficiency
H8	Health 8
HIV	Human immunodeficiency virus
IAVI	International AIDS Vaccine Initiative
ICESCR	International Covenant on Economic, Social and Cultural Rights
ICRC	International Committee of the Red Cross
IFFIm	International Finance Facility for Immunization
IHRs	International Health Regulations
ILO	International Labour Organization
IMF	International Monetary Fund
INGOs	International non-governmental organizations
IUATLD	International Union Against Tuberculosis and Lung Disease

MCH	Maternal Child Health
MDGs	Millennium Development Goals
MDR	Multi-drug resistant (TB)
NGO	Non-governmental organization
NTD	Neglected Tropical Disease
ODA	Official Development Assistance
OIHP	Office International d'Hygiene Publique
PAS	Para-amino salicylic acid
PDPPPs	Product Development Public-Private Partnerships
PEPFAR	President's Emergency Plan for AIDS Relief
PPPs	Public-private partnerships
SARS	Severe Acute Respiratory Syndrome
SIDA	Swedish International Development Cooperation Agency
SWAps	Sector-wide approaches
TB	Tuberculosis
TRIPs	Trade-related intellectual property rights
UN	United Nations
UNAIDS	Joint United Nations Programme on HIV/AIDS
UNDP	United Nations Development Programme
UNESCO	United Nations Educational, Scientific and Cultural Organization
UNFPA	United Nations Population Fund
UNHCR	United Nations High Commissioner for Refugees
UNICEF	United Nations Children's Fund
UNIFEM	United Nations Fund for Women
UNODC	United Nations Office on Drugs and Crime
USAID	United States Agency for International Development
WHA	World Health Assembly
WHO	World Health Organization
WTO	World Trade Organization
XDR	Extensively resistant (TB)

Introduction

- **Bringing health back in**
- **Understanding global health**
- **Structure of the book**

Global health matters. It matters to markets, states, individuals, and international institutions. Health is important to the ability of individuals to live more productive lives free from risk of their own pain, suffering or low self-esteem and that of their family and friends. State security, safety, and stability rests on keeping citizens healthy and protected from emerging global health threats or risks. Moreover, state economies are based on the production and labor force of healthy workers. Global health is integral to the growth and spread of markets in the reproduction of consumers and producers. Whether in terms of nutrition, ability to work, or susceptibility to disease, health continues to be the barometer of extreme poverty and inequality in the world. It remains at the cornerstone of questions of justice, equality, and rights. Such inequalities have become exacerbated as health risks, threats, and delivery have become globalized. Underpinning the United Nations' Millennium Development Goals (MDGs) and multiple World Bank strategies for growth and development is the need to secure the health—whether mental or physical—of populations. The increased movement of goods, people, and diseases across borders and changes to the climate and environment makes individual health a global concern and a multifarious, complex issue in which to govern.

Despite recognition that health matters, the provision of equitable health is problematic. Health provision across societies varies and often depends on who takes responsibility: the state, the individual, or the market. The primary function of any state or society is to secure the well-being of its citizens. Individuals are similarly concerned with their own personal health and that of their families and communities. The degree to which the state should provide treatment and education on health topics and threats, and to what extent and individual is capable of maintaining their own sufficient standard of health remains problematic. This contention rests on the ability of the state to provide basic services and capabilities and for individuals to have sufficient knowledge and wealth to maintain physical and mental well-being. Inequalities across society mean that health is more an asset that people can or cannot afford than a basic right or principle of our existence. The degree of such inequality varies between states and societies but globally the pattern of inequality takes on a North–South divide as inequalities become organized across and between states. It is awareness and a compulsion to address this inequality that has precipitated the emergence of a broad and complex system of global health governance.

Global health is a unique arena of governance that integrates scientists, medical practitioners, philanthropists, governments, and international institutions with grandmothers in local communities and self-styled celebrity advocates. Global health governance involves an amalgamation of various state, non-state, private, and public actors and as such has developed beyond the institutional role of the World Health Organization (WHO) and state-based ministries of health. In the most basic sense of the term global health governance refers to trans-border agreements or initiatives between states and/or non-state actors to the control of public health and infectious disease and the protection of people from health risks or threats. It is a fluid term that encompasses an ever-changing pattern of actors—both public and private, approaches, and priorities for those who are in the position to govern and those who are susceptible to poor health.

Global health governance is not a new phenomenon but one of the oldest forms of multilateral organization with its institutional origins preceding many intergovernmental organizations and governance systems. Structures of global health have emerged alongside increased state interdependency and a growth in world trade and the movement of goods and people. What is new about global health, however, is the accelerated impact trade, climate change, international finance, and security concerns have had on its governance and the flourishing of actors and arrangements to address and harness these issues to the benefit of better health for all. Global health is now the domain of finance ministries, international financial institutions, regional organizations, militaries, new funding initiatives based on evolved private–public partnerships, private philanthropy, celebrity endorsement, and business coalitions. These actors and initiatives center on the need to improve the mental and physical well-being of all individuals, specifically those living in the global south, and to secure populations in the global north from the spread of infectious disease. This is pursued through the reconstruction of health systems, the provision of medicine and treatment, the sharing of knowledge, and increasingly, the monitoring of disease and risk through surveillance systems. The emergence of these actors and initiatives makes global health governance a confusing phenomenon based on multiple relationships that represent a merger between health and non-health specific interventions.

The number of actors and initiatives involved in global health make its governance a balancing act between competing interests of the private and public sector, horizontal and vertical methods of intervention, individual liberties and state intervention, and global decision-making with decentralized implementation. This book provides a way of understanding this balancing act and how these differences manifest themselves into better or worse health outcomes. As such, this book is an introduction to understanding global health governance: who decides what, how, and for whom. It introduces global health governance by outlining the roles of and intersecting relationships between old and new actors, the different approaches to understanding global health, and how specific conceptions of the right to health and health as a public good underpin global policy and intervention. It focuses on a range of health concerns, with a specific focus on HIV/AIDS, tuberculosis, malaria, maternal health, neglected tropical disease, and health system strengthening. In so doing it considers how specific health issues or approaches are prioritized and why some are neglected and how institutions for global health have adapted, changed, or declined.

Bringing health back in

In the domestic context health is a vote winner for political parties, of significant importance to individuals, and placed "high" on the political agenda of governments and the populations they govern. Yet, *global* health policy has often been seen as an arena of "low" or "soft" politics that is somehow a side issue to more "hard" or "high" policy areas such as conflict, security, development, and the economy. Up until recently, health was seen to have little relevance to global politics and international relations but was sidelined to the domain of public health. In policy terms global health was governed by specific intergovernmental agencies with a primary focus on health, medical practitioners, and public health specialists. The last 20 years have seen wider recognition of the value of global health in both policy terms and academic research. This importance has gained greater currency in global policy-making strategies and agendas as global health has been identified both as a key benchmark for socio-economic development and a security threat. The result of this has been a growth in actors that engage in global health policy and the inclusion of health in defense and development strategies. Emerging from this growing recognition is a sophisticated and somewhat complicated system of global health governance that has brought health very much back on the political agenda as an issue of "high" global importance. How we can understand this form of governance, the approaches that underpin it, its relevance to global politics, and the actors and issues involved is the purpose of this book.

Understanding global health

A starting point to understanding what global health governance is to think about what is being governed. Health in the most basic sense of the term relates to the absence of illness or disease, or as behavior in terms of a healthy life and well-being[1] with a proper balance between body and mind.[2] The majority of global health interventions have centered on the management of public bads through disease control/elimination/eradication depending on the political and financial resources available.[3] Ultimately the method of control taken—that is, to eliminate, control, or eradicate—comes down to the socio-political commitment based on public interest, money, return, and political will.

Interventions into public health are typified as either or a combination of funding initiatives, high-profile policy statements and commitments, and project implementation of standalone health programs or health components of wider development strategies. These interventions tend to be either vertical in their focus on a specific disease or health issue, or horizontal in approaching global health systems more broadly and as part of wider infrastructure programs. Traditionally, these different types of intervention have been underpinned by a biomedical standpoint and approach to doing global health. This situates medical practitioners in a position of power that they are able to assert through claims to knowledge and expertise. For some this leads to a form of "medical imperialism" wherein the western biomedical model is applied regardless of cultural experience and local responses to illness.[4] Seeing health in biomedical terms encourages a degree of consumerism towards both preventative and curative interventions.[5] The biomedical approach assumes individuals to be vulnerable and somewhat helpless in addressing their own health concerns or individual weaknesses independent of medicine and medical practitioners. The biomedical approach argues that ill-health is the result of bad choices by individuals not of the inequalities within society that help facilitate poor health.[6] Health sectors grow in direct relation to the growth of social needs and processes of capitalist accumulation.[7] These arguments point to two different understandings as to the role of doctors in the provision of health services and delivery: on the one hand, doctors and public health workers are driven by the need to help people and make the world a healthier place; on the other, medical professionals are driven by wealth, knowledge, and status.[8]

For many, this model of biomedical health intervention remains the case for global health governance, with biomedicine defining those issues that are important and how they are addressed[9] and creating a market for the production of different treatment and methods of delivery. Methods of delivering global health are interesting here, as on the one hand, global health governance is explicitly linked to processes of global inequality and socio-economic determinants, while on the other, policy and provision is framed in the context of individual responsibility. Moreover, the problem of "Doctor knows best" is positioned against that of the community, the economist, the United Nations (UN) agency, and the specialized state department within the terrain of global health governance. The result of which is the governance of more than just health and illness of individuals within a state but the governance of behavior, trade, aid, inequality, gender, and security. For many, this broad remit of global health governance is the direct result of globalization and the shift from "international" to "global" health.

The dominant discourse on global health governance has been to conceptualize it in relation to global inequalities seen to arise from processes of neoliberal globalization that emerged in the late 1970s.[10] It is argued that this period marked the shift from "international" to "global" health governance[11] as health issues and the ability of states to address these issues extended beyond state boundaries and territories.[12] Neoliberalism in regard to global health governance is used in the most generic sense of the term, that of a global economic process that encompasses significant political and social reform based on the primacy of the market, competition, minimal state intervention, and private sector efficiency. The outcome of neoliberal globalization for global health has occupied much debate that can generally be categorized into five areas: i) impact on state delivery of health services; ii) growth of non-state actors; iii) population movement and the spread of disease; iv) changes to food production and consumption; and v) trade, patents, and access to medicine.

Emphasis on the market, the role of the private sector, and minimal state funding for health saw a reduction in public investment and involvement in the provision of better health for all throughout the 1980s and 1990s. This was evident in many countries in North America and Europe and was spread throughout middle-income countries and less developed countries. Economic "shock therapy" towards post-Soviet states and controversial structural adjustment packages promoted by the World Bank and International Monetary Fund (IMF) in developing countries saw a curtailment of health spending in the 1980s and early 1990s. Such packages emphasized the rapid deployment and investment of funds in developing countries to stimulate growth, principally within the private sector, on the condition that states reformed their economies on market-based lines. Key to privatization practices was the introduction of user fees for health services. The result of which was healthcare being seen as less of a right, but more "in terms of privatization potential"[13] where health services are a commodity. The role of structural adjustment not only reformed healthcare along neoliberal lines, but saw the emergence of international financial institutions such as the World Bank and the World Trade Organization (WTO) as central actors within global health governance. Privatized healthcare and a reduced role of the state led to a growth in non-state actors filling the gaps of health provision. These actors have come to act in partnership with or in replacement of public investment.

In reducing barriers to the flow of trade, goods and services, globalization has facilitated a shift in labor patterns that has had a direct impact on the healthcare of workers, the spread of disease and health resources. For some, globalization has led to a new international division of labor based on rapid labor exchange, economic insecurity for individuals, intensive use of labor, and a race to the bottom in terms of labor standards, the result of which has been poor health outcomes and standards of healthcare for workers.[14] Labor migration arising from shifts in employment patterns from rural communities to capital cities and less restriction on the movement of people has been a key factor in the transmission of infectious disease across borders and in-state. Moreover, in some countries greater flexibility in the globalized world of work has led to shortages of health workers such as doctors, radiologists, and nurses. Conversely, with changes to labor patterns having an impact on ill-health, ill-health affects the ability of individuals to work. As Dreze and Sen argue, all labor power rests on health as a basic necessity for life.[15]

Where health inequalities exist they have the most impact in cities.[16] Cities have the "urban advantage" of having more health centers and advanced resources, and the "urban penalty" of increased susceptibility to poor health.[17] Globalization has compounded these two factors by stimulating urbanization as growth in trade and services requires a shift away from more rural forms of employment. Half of the world's population live in cities[18] and the rise in the global city as networks for people, trade, capital, commodities, communication, and transportation makes them networks for disease transmission. A key example of the impact of this was the outbreak of SARS in 2003 where "the fluid mobility of microbes that thrive in the connectivity of globalized urban environments" was at its most obvious.[19]

Perhaps the starkest evidence of the unequal nature of globalization has been its impact on food production and the growth of two opposing but inter-related health concerns: obesity and malnutrition. Global production and trade in food and agriculture is not a new phenomenon, and has been central to concerns of public health for centuries. What is new about globalization and food is the scale of change and the magnitude of choice that has led to poor quality diets, obesity, under-nutrition, and diet-related chronic diseases. Changes to food systems have altered both the amount and the quality of food produced around the world that has led to a change of diet and instead of leading to greater provision for all has led to a distinction between haves and have nots, and diets that are high in saturated fat, salt, and sugar. Combined with changes in the world trade system that maintains a system of agricultural subsidies in developed countries to the detriment of agricultural production in developing countries, global production and trade has a direct impact on the health of the world's population. It is this same world trade system which maintains patent protection in ways that, as Chapters 2 and 4 show, can distort access to medicine and treatment in developing countries.

Combined, these factors have led to a growth in health inequality based on unequal distribution of disease relating to poverty, economic insecurity, and marginalization, with any potential benefits of globalization still coming into question. Health has not become available to all, but a disparity between rich and poor, and hence those that can afford it.[20] For many public health experts, the literature on globalization tells us a lot about how inequalities in global health arise and are perpetuated by specific systems of the global political economy.[21] It is the relationship between such inequality and globalization that marks the shift from international to global health governance, and as such underpins common understandings of the term. However, even though these inequalities suggest much about the problems and emerging concerns in relation to public health and their causes it reveals little about global health's *governance*. Governance in this regard is often used in reference to the impact of the international financial institutions' structural adjustment policies of the 1980s and the early 1990s and the role of non-state actors. Global health governance has become a much broader and encompassing term that relates to specific processes, approaches, procedures, and policy directives organized by a myriad of actors and initiatives. Hence, even though globalization stimulated much of this activity and the emergence of these actors, global health has entered a post-globalization phase wherein its governance represents and advances these changes and shifts within the broader terrain of global health.

Current structures of global health governance are seen as organized around competition, differing discourses on health,[22] and bureaucracy which makes these mechanisms "inadequate at best, and dysfunctional at worst."[23] Despite this inadequacy, understandings of global health governance are centered on the need to improve it, and the notion that it can be improved as current trends presents an "opportunity as never before."[24] Suggestions as to how to improve global health governance follow three lines of argument: the first reverts back to the association between global health governance and neoliberalism and health inequalities that suggest governance can only be effective if the structures of political economy that underpin it are addressed;[25] the second is to build upon global health as a public good and develop shared norms to coordinate and unify the actors and processes that make up global health governance;[26] the third is to recognize the potential of new actors and strengthen existing health-specific institutions. Key to this has been the rhetoric and importance attributed to innovation.

What these three approaches have in common is that global health is seen as something that is vital for economic stability, prosperity, peace and security, and a global good. It is thus something to be valued and strived for. Moreover each of these approaches agree that global health governance is in need of change: either a reverting back to public institutions such as the WHO, or an expansion in the types of institutions and new approaches to how we understand and tackle global health, or a combination of both. It is how to approach health, which health concerns to prioritize, how to frame issues, and the institutions best placed to do so that make global health governance so complicated and confusing. This book unravels some of these complications by outlining the different approaches, actors, and issues involved in global health governance as a means of going forward in promoting better health for all.

Structure of the book

The aim of this book is to understand the conceptual underpinnings to how global health is governed, the multiple actors and funding initiatives that constitute the core of global health governance, and how such actors and approaches have been applied to specific health concerns over others. The book provides an overview of actors, issues, and processes, and a specialist understanding of the governance of HIV/AIDS, tuberculosis, malaria, and neglected health. The book begins by building on this Introduction in exploring the ways in which we can understand global health governance in Chapter 1. Broader inclusion of public health specialists, economists, lawyers, and social scientists has seen a shift in how global health is approached and understood, and what falls into the remit of governance. Such inclusion has seen the rise of rights-based approaches to health based on ideas of equity and access to basic capabilities and the need to involve multiple sectors of society in governing health issues. This chapter first explains what is meant by inequity, health as a global public good, and the right to health. Second, the chapter focuses on what is multisectoralism and how it marks a movement away from biomedical approaches to governance. The third section of the chapter explores the role of securitizing health and biopolitical control as a means of identifying specific health issues as threats or risks. In so doing, the chapter provides the basis of understanding the role of issue-framing within global health governance as a means of eliciting wider funds, creating political will out of fear or empathy, and emphasizing specific health issues to the neglect of others.

Chapter 2 provides the "nuts and bolts" of what the traditional institutions of global health governance are, key frameworks and treaties associated with the evolution of global health governance, and their relative successes and failings. The chapter does so by focusing first on the role of the state and bilateral assistance in the delivery and provision of healthcare within the domestic and global. The chapter then considers the formation of global responses to health during the "golden age" of biomedical discovery in the nineteenth century to the formation of the International Sanitary Regulations and the Office International d'Hygiene Publique in the early twentieth century. The chapter traces how these antecedents contributed to the idea of first the League of Nations Health Organization and then the WHO. The chapter explores the role and structure of the WHO as well as its approach to global health and challenges to its role as the lead agency for global health. The WHO's role as the lead agency for global health has been challenged by UN specialized agencies such as the United Nations Children's Fund (UNICEF), the United Nations Development Program (UNDP), the United Nations Population Fund (UNFPA), and financial institutions such as the World Bank, WTO, and the IMF. The chapter outlines the role of these institutions within global health before focusing on non-governmental organizations (NGOs) and private philanthropic organizations such as the Rockefeller Foundation and the Bill and Melinda Gates Foundation.

Global health governance has been marked by the emergence of multiple forms of funding, new institutions, and partnerships emerging from civil society and the private sector. Chapter 3 makes sense of these actors by outlining their purpose, influence, and impact upon the delivery of healthcare and governance of global health. The chapter explores the evolving role of the G8 and G20 in global health, and initiatives such as the Global Fund to Fight HIV/AIDS, Tuberculosis and Malaria arising from this role. The chapter then focuses on the emergence of new forms of public–private partnership and financing mechanisms such as the International AIDS Vaccine Initiative (IAVI), the Global Alliance for Vaccines and Immunisation (GAVI), and UNITAID. Beyond new financing mechanisms, the chapter explores the shift in delivery of better global health towards the community and decentralized governance structures. The chapter finishes by outlining the growth in celebrity involvement with global health governance— both in terms of charismatic leaders within global health institutions and high-profile musicians, athletes, and actors.

Chapter 4 focuses upon three diseases that have generated considerable support and attention under the shift from "international" to "global" health: HIV/AIDS, tuberculosis, and malaria. It does so by briefly outlining what they are and how they are governed, and how the trends and institutions discussed in the previous chapters manifest themselves in practice. The chapter then discusses why these three diseases have become "big" and occupy most attention through interventions and finance, and how they have stimulated the creation of multiple partnerships and initiatives within global health governance. The chapter assesses the outcome, successes, and failures of global interventions into these three areas in turn, and what these outcomes imply for the effectiveness of global health interventions and how they help us characterize its governance.

The prioritization of specific diseases has seen the neglect and sidelining of other health concerns and priorities. Chapter 5 broadens the scope of neglect beyond that of neglected tropical disease to consider other health concerns that have been neglected, that of women's health,

health systems and infrastructure. The chapter does so by first providing an overview of neglected tropical diseases: what they are, why they are neglected, and recent challenges to such neglect. The chapter then broadens its focus to women's health and the role of maternal health as the neglected development goal. The chapter explores how despite a rapid increase in efforts to address the problem of maternal health, gendered approaches to health and the experiences of women remain sidelined within wider structures of global health governance. The chapter finishes by engaging with the contentious debate over vertical and horizontal interventions into healthcare, and whether health system strengthening constitutes a form of neglected health governance. In so doing, the chapter re-positions the role of neglect in global health governance: what it means for institutions both old and new, and how political will and interest is constructed in regard to specific health interventions.

Chapter 6 draws together the main findings of Chapters 1–5 to articulate how global health governance can be understood; what the institutions, structures, and approaches are, and how we can make sense of this. The chapter argues that global health governance can best be understood as a balancing act between different dichotomies of centralized decision-making and decentralized intervention, public and private approaches to and understandings of health, and the issue of rights and responsibilities of individuals and states. It is the lack of balance between these dichotomies that makes global health governance so complex, unequal, and confused and leads to the key questions posed by this book: who or what governs global health? To what outcome and for whom?

1 Approaches to global health governance

- **Inequity, justice, and global public goods**
- **Right to health**
- **Multisectoralism**
- **Health as a security concern**
- **Health governance as biopolitics**
- **Conclusion**

Central to the governance of global health and the institutional mechanisms organized within it are the conceptual approaches that direct how certain health issues are addressed, defined, and prioritized. Approaches to health governance have changed rapidly over the last fifty years. Typically biomedical models of health interventions have dominated the terrain of how we understand global health and how it is approached and practiced. However, the increasingly globalized nature of health has required a wider recognition of the socio-economic determinants of poor health and the need to balance biomedical approaches with that of human rights and wider participation in delivering health services beyond medical practitioners. Global health has come to constitute a development concern, a barometer of global inequality, and a security threat. Each of these framings of health has had an impact on global health policy: how it is addressed, how specific issues come on to the global agenda, levels of public and private sector involvement, and how institutions have positioned health and disease in global and local spaces.

This chapter builds on the shift from international to global health outlined in the Introduction. In so doing it considers the following approaches to global health governance: inequity and health as a public good, the right to health, multisectoralism, health as a security concern, and health as biopolitics. It outlines what is meant by each of these approaches, how they correspond to policy and practice, and what they mean for global health governance.

Inequity, justice, and global public goods

Health interventions have always been underpinned by debate over how to provide the best achievable healthcare for the largest number of the population whilst maintaining standards of care, the rights of the individual, and advances in medical research. The provision of health for all reflects rights and responsibilities basic to any social contract between those who deliver and receive care. This social contract can be seen in the Hippocratic Oath taken by medical practitioners to the modeling of how to run health systems effectively. As with recent changes in public health interventions, ethics and how to address inequalities within global health have come to the fore of our approach to public health. According to Tarantola *et al.*, the new public health movement that associates health with development processes and change within the global political economy has put the notion of rights, access to public goods, and the need to address global inequalities at the heart of this agenda.[1] Central to that is the framing of health within wider commitments to reducing poverty. Health remains the ultimate barometer of poverty, well-being, and relative deprivation, and there remains an important rationale that economic growth, political peace, and stability will only occur within healthy populations. Health and life expectancy continue to be directly related to social class and wealth.[2] Hence approaches to global health interventions have become cognizant of inequalities and inequities and the need to address them.

A basic definition of health inequities can be those "differences (in health) which are unnecessary and unavoidable but, in addition, are also considered unfair and unjust."[3] Health inequity is often seen to be driven by risky behavior, healthcare provision, structural change, and the clustering of risk factors. In practice, for health this means tackling specific health issues and diseases in the form of vertical interventions, or more horizontal health system strengthening, and broadening the remit of public health out to include the structural determinants of inequity. In contrast, health equity refers to the absence of avoidable differences among populations defined socially, economically, demographically, or geographically. Hence, health (in)equity is based on a normative understanding of what is considered to be fair or just. Any intervention to combat health inequity is thus underpinned by wider debates on distributive justice and the contention over equality of opportunity and equality of outcome.

For Amartya Sen, distributive health justice rests on the "capabilities" argument that there are a number of capabilities essential to the health of individuals. Individuals should be provided with these basic capabilities: once provided, it becomes the individual's responsibility or choice as to how they use or disregard these capabilities. According to Sen, "health is among the most important conditions of human life and a critically significant constituent of human capabilities which we have reason to value,"[4] health becomes a central capability for an individual's ability to function,[5] and hence the provision of social justice. Inequalities may arise from individual choice, but inequities in health are centered upon unequal access to these capabilities. It thus becomes the responsibility of states to "level up" and provide these basic capabilities to address inequalities. Although he does not directly address health,[6] distributive health justice and the capabilities argument has often been discussed in the context of John Rawls' egalitarianism. In principle, provision of basic capabilities should give rise to what Rawls sees as "fair equality of opportunity."[7] As such, health as a capability becomes a right underpinned by a normative understanding of distributive justice, which for a just society to exist health is a basic function, capability, or a global public good. The problem is that when applying such a principle to practice, questions arise over which capabilities function as "basic" capabilities, who or what should provide for them and at what cost.

Health inequity and renewed focus on the capabilities argument has led to the labeling of health as a global public good, in that it should be non-excludable—no one should be excluded from accessing good health—and non-rivalrous—in that one person's health does not restrict another's. Health is a *global* public good in that its benefits are, or should be, universal across sovereign borders, people, and generations.[8] Increased interdependency between states and global issues has transposed health from a private good, that is, of which the individual is the prime beneficiary, to being public with multiple external effects on the global economy, environment, and society.[9] According to Chen *et al.*, it is these global "externalities" that see the shift of health from a private good to a global public good and the indivisibility of health as a positive sum game in which all must benefit, with one's health not detracting from another's.[10]

The non-rivalrous and non-excludable nature of public goods can make their supply and consumption problematic.[11] For Kaul *et al.*, public goods tend to be under-provided and over-consumed.[12] Access to global public goods may depend on indirect cost, governance and control, change, and geography resulting in individuals being excluded.[13] For example, health and knowledge are both considered global public goods, yet health knowledge is excludable through patent laws, product location, and the infrastructure delivering such knowledge.[14]

Such public goods depend on the distinction between the non-rivalrous and non-excludable nature of *both* production and consumption.[15] Provision of global public goods by the free market generates problems and concerns of free-riding that in turn result in under-supply.[16] Framing health as non-excludable or non-rivalrous in turn can lead to problems over who covers the cost and responsibility of their provision, what cost and to whom.[17] Non-excludability can lead to the sidelining, or exclusion of health interventions that do not apply to the whole population, for example child health or women's health, and moreover create a stalemate on any health interventions that undergo the existential question as to what impact they may or may not have on future generations. Thus, for Woodward and Smith, an alternative approach to health as a global public good would be to stress the degree to which goods exhibit "publicness *across national boundaries*" in which it is irrational to exclude individuals and, crucially, "irrespective of whether that nation contributes to its financing."[18]

Approaches to health as a basic capability or a global public good act as normative guides as to how health should be considered and how inequalities within healthcare should be addressed. However, they are not only thought-exercises posing questions and ideas of justice, but translate into real policy outcomes through the emergence of multisectoral agendas for health and global commitments to health as a human right through recognition of the right to health. It is the problems, contradictions, and debates over social justice and fairness within these capabilities and public-goods-based arguments that make the terrain of global public health provision so problematic in terms of responsibilities, action, and who funds them.

Right to health

The association between health, distributive justice, and global public goods has led to a broadening of the health agenda to include rights and multisectoral inclusion of non-health practitioners and approaches to combating health inequity. The first example of this has been the development of the United Nations "right to health." The right to health refers to the right of everyone to the enjoyment of the highest attainable standard of physical and mental health, established by the United Nations (UN) Commission of Human Rights resolutions 2002/31 and 2004/27 and extended by Human Rights Council 6/29.[19] The right to health is an explicit recognition of the relationship between health and human rights, and their broader association with health inequity. As special rapporteur on the right to health 2002–8,

Paul Hunt, argues, health is adversely affected by human rights abuses, specific health policies can be in violation of human rights, and in turn ill-health and vulnerability to ill-health can be reduced by greater awareness of human rights.[20]

Rights-based interventions should enhance participation, empowerment, accountability, and crucially in regard to health equity, social justice.[21] The right to health has the following main features. First, it is an inclusive right, based on non-discrimination and equal treatment of acceptable and good quality. It cannot be bought or sold. Non-discrimination and equality are fundamental principles of human rights laws and are thus intrinsic to the right to health.[22] Second, it contains freedoms and entitlements, in that individuals have the right to prevention, treatment, and control of disease, and should be free from non-consensual medical treatment or experimentation. Individuals should be free to control the health of their body and be active and informed participants in decision-making on their health. States must not directly violate an individual's right to health, and must further monitor non-state and private actors to this end.[23] Hence, third, the right to health should be accountable and involve multiple forms of participation from individuals, states, and the international community. Fourth, the right to health is not the right to be healthy or an abstract ideal. It has short-term aims, resources, and guiding principles, and is progressive in character.[24] The right to health is not just an abstract concept but has systems and structures in which to operationalize its objectives.

The purpose of the right to health is to take a rights-based approach to health interventions, applied by human rights treaties and mechanisms. The right to health is implemented through a variety of international, national, and regional laws that clarify the role of different actors in terms of delivery and monitoring.[25] In terms of domestic law, the right to health is enshrined in 60 national constituencies, and 115 state constitutions, and multiple sources of regional law and regional human rights treaties.[26] States are also bound to multiple sources of international law, most notably the International Covenant on Economic, Social and Cultural Rights (ICESCR), article 12, which safeguards the right to health. Article 12 stipulates the need to take steps to reduce infant mortality and child development; improve environmental and industrial hygiene; prevent, treat, and control epidemic, endemic, occupational, and other diseases; create conditions that assure medical services and medical attention in the event of sickness. The broad range of health concerns and their inter-relationship with other human and labor rights and development issues means that the right to health is also enshrined in other international treaties[27] and public health policies.[28] Those states that recognize the right to health commit to core obligations: respect, protect, fulfill, and progression towards realization. In practice, this requires states to provide the essential bases of primary care, food, housing, sanitation, and the adoption and implementation of a national health plan.[29] Enshrining the right to health in domestic law gives individuals the right to pursue complaints or legal decisions within national courts, and hence affords them the opportunity to hold states to account.[30] Making the right to health work in practice thus rests on individual participation in regard to the ability of individuals to make decisions as well as how they hold states to account.

Accountability and the adherence to the international, regional, and state legislation show some of the flaws of the right to health approach. Whilst the approach takes broad steps to addressing health inequities and is keen to have a tangible basis, in many ways it is a dead-letter regime that has the appearance of political commitment and will but little practical realization of it. For example, a topical problem with the right to health has been its relationship with other forms of international law, most notably international trade law such as the trade-related intellectual property rights (TRIPs) (see Chapter 2 for further detail). Under TRIPs, states "can adopt measures necessary to protect public health" and restrict patents "if they pose a threat to human life."[31] However, in practice the realization of this has been problematic, and often patent laws supersede the right to health, as often trade interests take precedence over population health, specifically health as a human right. The provision of the right to health goes back to a central contention with the capabilities argument that underpins it: who provides such capabilities. In the national context, the provision of capabilities rests on the social contract between a state and its citizens, thus the state should provide. However, in a global system of inequality the argument becomes less clear. Thus the right to health requires a mix of state and international support, yet the onus rests on the state and state responsibility. Approaches to health based on the right to health therefore become underpinned by contentions over the need for state responsibility offset by state capability; the need for global assistance in providing state support; the relationship between trade and health; and how best to make states obey international law.

Multisectoralism

The need for participation and accountability in the right to health and inclusion in delivering health services has facilitated the rise of an alternative model of health intervention: multisectoralism. Multi-sectoralism, or multisectorality, refers to the inclusion of multiple actors—state, non-state, community-based, globally-based, regional, private, and public—in the provision and decision-making of health-care initiatives. The purpose of this is to recognize the inter-relationship of health with multiple sectors of state-based activity, development, and inequality; and to increase participation and accountability within global health. The concept of multisectoralism has its origins in United Nations Development Programme (UNDP) and World Health Organization (WHO) approaches to health. The UNDP introduced the term multisectoralism in the late 1980s to acknowledge the health and non-health aspects of health issues and the need to engage multiple actors in addressing the socio-economic dimensions of ill-health such as poverty, inequality, gender, and stigma.[32] For the UNDP, promoting better health outcomes would involve multiple actors from multiple sectors, with the state at the core of interventions. Multisectoralism fitted within the WHO's over-arching approach to the right to health and inclusion of non-governmental organizations (NGOs) and other non-state based actors in public health interventions. Multisectoralism thus came to mean the involvement of multiple state, non-state, public and private actors from both health and non-health sectors to incorporate the joined up nature of health interventions with broader efforts towards poverty eradication. However, under the UNDP and the WHO it remained little more than rhetoric and an ideal than common practice.

Multisectoralism was fully operationalized as a health strategy by the World Bank in the mid 1990s through sector-wide approaches (or SWAps) to health. The Bank used the SWAp as its main framework for addressing a number of health concerns. The appeal of such an approach for the Bank was it acknowledged the need to respond to the various socio-economic and multisectoral drivers of poor health and the linkages between health and development. The core features of the practical application of such an approach were to first apply it to a specific health concern and then either remove the issue from the core responsibility of the ministry of health in a specific country to a sepa-rate political office or create a standalone agency within the health ministry. This would heighten the presence of the issue and create greater space for wider participation from non-health specific parts of government, and crucially, non-state actors in the form of civil society organizations and the private sector. Multiple organizations would then be involved in the planning and implementation of an issue-specific strategic plan, based on clearly defined and commonly agreed upon roles and responsibilities. The Bank's holistic, sector-wide approach to global health has seen a prioritization of multiple aspects of government systems within developing countries, grouped together under an umbrella coordinating agency located at the center of government, nominally the office of the president/prime minister.

Multisectoralism is not only limited to health interventions within the state, but can also be applied to global coordination efforts. As Chapters 2 and 3 will show, global health governance encompasses a myriad of institutions and actors that are often overlapping in their roles, and cluster around specific health issues. New institutions engaged in global health issues are not necessarily health organizations per se, but address health as part of a wider agenda of sustainable development and poverty alleviation. These actors exist within the broad framework of multisectoralism and the recognition that multiple actors are important to health interventions but need to be coordinated under the aegis of multisectoralism. Coordination is thus at the cornerstone of multisectoralism and the practice of doing global health governance.

The term "sector-wide" approach has now been replaced by an overarching commitment to multisectoralism. This can be seen in the existing projects on HIV/AIDS, neglected disease, and emerging high-profile World Bank projects such as maternal health and infant mortality. The value placed on multisectoral health interventions by the World Bank and UN agencies highlights how non-health ministry specific interventions within the state are commonplace and prioritized. Sector-wide approaches and regional cooperation have previously been a central part of global health governance; however, activities within the state have been firmly located within the health sector. Despite organizations such as the WHO continuing to emphasize health system strengthening, multisectoralism is moving the delivery and planning for health interventions away from the state towards the inclusion of multiple non-state actors. Multisectoralism has shifted the biomedical paradigm that has previously defined global health governance and applied "the new public health" positioning health as a development objective into practice.

Health as a security concern

In somewhat contention to rights-based and multisectoral approaches to global health governance has been the association between health and security. The need to address global health has long been justified on the basis of security, protection of populations, and the aversion of risk. This need was at its height at the end of the Second World War, with the WHO being established to promote peace and stability through the provision of better standards of global health. Health is seen as both a preventer of war, and war and violent conflict as a clear indicator of disability-adjusted life years lost.[33] Wars increase the rate of mortality and morbidity among civilian populations, destroy health infrastructure, reduce access to basic services, for example, food and water, divert money to be spent on health to military uses, and increase the vulnerability of certain populations.[34] The lack of infrastructure and social upheaval caused by war exacerbate these health outcomes. Inability to address these concerns can lead to further civil unrest and instability within a state, greater mobility of the main vectors of disease (human bodies) and changes to the environment. The antecedents and processes of institutionalization make the relationship between health and security hard to avoid and intrinsic to any wider policymaking in global health governance. Since 2001 there has been a resurgent interest in global health and security in response to new perceived threats of infectious disease such as HIV and its relationship with state and global security; anthrax and bioterror in the post 9/11 world; pandemic outbreaks of influenza such as severe acute respiratory syndrome (SARS) and H1N1; and a shift to non-state-based but human models of security. Health has become a security concern because of its effects on the global economy and poverty, the susceptibility of militaries and peacekeepers to disease[35] and the perception of risk and new concerns of biosecurity. The association of health and security concerns has a galvanizing function; it makes states interact because of the *global threat* of health, however, this threat is not necessarily warranted and can lead to further problems in how we address global health initiatives.

The role of health as a means of promoting peace and security embedded within the post-War order became latent throughout the twentieth century with the emergence of rights-based approaches to health and the labeling of health as an issue of "soft" or "low" politics in the context of the Cold War. During this period, health and state security was only considered in regard to the Vietnam War and the threat of bioweapons. It was not until the discovery of the HIV virus, its global prevalence rate, and the cause of infection that health once again became an important issue for national security and state stability. The main threat HIV/AIDS has for state stability is primarily in relation to a state's army. Levels of HIV prevalence in countries in sub-Saharan Africa are often cited as being higher within the state military than the civilian population.[36] This has outcomes for how combat ready a state is, its vulnerability to both internal and external challenges, the cost of keeping a state's armed forces healthy, and the need to retain skilled service personnel. Beyond the military, HIV weakens the economy, labor relations and development outcomes for poor states which can foster wider civil strife. According to Singer[37] increased vulnerability caused by HIV heightens aggression as people fight over limited resources and become more susceptible to criminal activity. This is a particular risk for the 15 million children orphaned by AIDS.

The turning point for this relationship is often cited as being the 2001 UN Security Council and General Assembly special sessions on HIV/AIDS and its impact on peace and security. Six months after its initial meeting, the Security Council passed Resolution 1308 that outlined the potential risk to UN peacekeepers deployed in areas of high HIV prevalence, how violence exacerbated HIV infection, and crucially how HIV/AIDS "may pose a risk to stability and security." This meeting was met with similar rhetoric from the World Bank, African heads of state, state officials,[38] and the academic community trying to make sense of this new security threat and its relationship to models of human security. However, there is increased recognition that this threat has been somewhat over-stated, and moreover, for some has been more about galvanizing resources for HIV/AIDS initiatives than framing the epidemic as a serious security concern. McInnes has argued that there is no empirical evidence to suggest HIV/AIDS has led to an increased risk of conflict in a country, that the numbers of military personnel infected have been exaggerated, and the need for caution in over-stating this relationship.[39] These concerns point to wider problems of increasingly "securitized" health and the threat to public health interventions these frames can have. Securitizing health can often be seen to exist at the cost of rights-based approaches to health, and the perpetuation of risk and fear. This is most clearly seen in the second issue pertinent to health and security: biosecurity.

Biosecurity refers to the need to safeguard against the threat of biological weapons and naturally occurring infectious disease.[40] Biosecurity interventions are based on the need to protect states and their citizens from the threat of bioterrorism—"the infliction of harm by the intentional manipulation of living micro-organisms or their natural products for hostile purposes"—and bioweapons such as bacteria, viruses, fungi, and toxins.[41] Biological weapons are some of the oldest forms of weaponry in warfare, they are adaptable to change and pose new security risks. According to Fidler and Gostin, despite the 1925 Geneva Protocol banning the use of bacteriological agents in warfare, there is growing suggestion that security and health specialists need to come together to contain and protect against very real biosecurity threats.[42] The threat of biosecurity is made real by recent events such as the 2002 anthrax letters in the United States and the 1995 Sarin gas attack in Tokyo. In each case, the state responded to these threats by establishing surveillance and preparedness systems. However, an increasingly inter-dependent world has made these threats more global and less easy to predict in terms of where bioweapons are being developed, who they are used by, who they are used against, and when.

Global policy responses to the supposed biosecurity threat have been less forthcoming. For Kellman this is because of the fragmented nature of decision-making within global health governance, and confusion over the changing nature of science,[43] whereas for others, this could be because the threat of biosecurity is over-stated and funds to combat it would be diverted away from alternative health concerns. Despite this, proponents of the risk of bioviolence, such as Kellman and Fidler, advocate the need to include prevention, resistance, preparation, and non-proliferation strategies into wider agendas for global health. Pre-vention of this kind would then be met with response interventions through a growth in public health financing.[44] Fidler and Gostin sug-gest such initiatives would be coordinated by a "concert mechanism" that combines security and health governance structures that promote and uphold the rule of law through a convention on biological weap-ons[45] such as a joint WHO-Interpol operation or three specific bodies within the UN.[46]

Questions over the threat of biosecurity and how to address such threats are underpinned by a contention between security and public health concerns. Even though the two are often conceived of as inter-dependent, there is a distinction between security expertise for doing health, and public health expertise for doing security. What we again see within the security approach to health is the stretching of public health beyond its narrow biomedical confines.[47] Biosecurity is framed as presenting a challenge for global health governance to respond to. For any response to biosecurity to work, global health governance has to be at the center, for it has the scientific and biomedical expertise and surveillance systems necessary to combat such threats.

The degree to which global health governance has responded to this challenge and how it occupies, or does not occupy, this central role rests on debates as to how real the biosecurity threat is and the pro-blems associated with securitizing health. For some the securitization of health is now complete, yet for others such as McInnes and Lee, questions remain as to whose security, whose risk and what issues the current agenda prioritizes.[48] Securitizing health has come to be more about changing state and individual behavior and changes to the global political economy[49] than protecting against risk and new health threats. McInnes and Lee argue that the framing of the health-security nexus has skewed the public health agenda so that those health concerns that are not identified as a high security concern do not receive adequate attention. The result for them is that public health no longer becomes an end in itself.[50] Taken to its far-reaching conclusion, securitizing health issues such as HIV/AIDS can, according to Elbe, lead to a "new biopolitical racism" of the healthy and non-healthy, in which those people who are HIV-positive may be segregated from communities or left to die by states.[51] In many ways the securitization of health and the health-security nexus are over-stated; public health experts are not interested in security concerns, and security experts are less interested in health.[52] Specific infectious diseases become securitized, but global health in general remains free from such labeling.

Health governance as biopolitics

The framing of health as a security concern and the ensuing need for surveillance, preparedness, and monitoring of perceived health risks can all be framed within the understanding of global health governance as a form of biopolitics. Emanating from debate about the securitization of HIV/AIDS and the perception of risk,[53] biopolitics can be applied to multiple health concerns, and the governance mechanisms that have emerged to combat or manage them. According to Elbe, biopolitics principally refers to Foucault's definition of the term as the extension of politics and the political beyond conflict, the economy and redistribution of wealth towards an over-arching concern for monitoring and shaping the biological characteristics of populations as living beings rather than political subjects.[54] Foucault distinguishes biopolitics from biopower and anatomo-politics. Biopolitics refers to the control of an individual's biological existence. Anatomo-politics indicates those political interventions addressing "man-as-body," that is, interventions that target the human body to make it more productive or passive. On the other hand, biopolitics refers to those interventions or political strategies that focus on "man-as-species" and address biological trends within the wider population, or at the population level, for example, birth rates and death rates. Biopower as power over life evolves through anatomo-politics targeting the human body, and biopolitics that organize power and govern life.[55] This conditioning and control of "man-as-body" and "man-as-species" was, for Foucault, indispensable to capitalist development, as any processes of production, principally the industrial revolution of the eighteenth century would not be possible without "the controlled insertion of bodies" into that process through the anatomo-politics of making the body more productive, and the biopolitical dimension of segregation and hierarchization.[56] For Foucault, sex is the "deployment of sexuality organized by power in its grip on bodies," their pleasure, energy, and force.[57] It is thus intrinsic to the expression and discursive terrain of biopolitics.

Whilst global health governance can be seen to engage in each of these three Foucauldian domains—biopolitics, anatomo-politics, and biopower—it is the focus on surveillance, monitoring, and change in population behavior as a global whole that makes biopolitics a relevant concept to understanding such governance. Biopolitics can be applied as a means of understanding global health governance in the following ways: its antecedents in the eighteenth century; current trends towards disease surveillance; the narrowing of knowledge; and risk. As Chapter 2 outlines, current structures of global health governance have their origins in the "golden age" of public health in the nineteenth century. For Foucault, it was this period that marked the emergence of biopolitical power with the development of surveillance systems, demography, and epidemiology concerned with population monitoring and control.[58] The central concern of the rulers was the body and sexuality of the ruled "to ensure the strength, endurance, and secular proliferation of that body" with class consciousness resting on the "affirmation" of the body.[59] For some this concern with the body and sexuality to maintain productivity and self-awareness continues to underpin global health governance; with inequality between the ruled and rulers as being the divide between the healthy and the non-healthy, and the need to govern the body as a means of promoting productivity and growth as a means of development and security. This is done through surveillance of population growth and the emergence and "threat" of new diseases, and the targeting of specific diseases, most notably HIV/AIDS, as having a detrimental effect on development and security. As Elbe has argued, governing global health thus becomes concerned with governing the body and sexuality through data, surveillance, and social interventions into monitoring the activity of the body.[60]

In governing the body, sex, and sexuality becomes a discourse annexed "to a field of rationality" that is historically bound to a logic of desire.[61] Discourse and knowledge becomes a central element of global health governance in what knowledge is prioritized and that which is sidelined within a "specific field of truth."[62] Public health interventions in the nineteenth century promoted the "healthy norm" of individual behavior[63] and a "universal truth" surrounding sex that facilitated suspicion and questions within wider society and led to individuals fearing sex.[64] Knowledge thus became divisive within and between individuals, with individuals becoming ignorant of themselves and their bodies.[65] Current structures of global health governance are imbued with a specific knowledge surrounding sex, how it is practiced, how it should be practiced, and its relationship with disease and population control. It has thus come to be feared or problematized in a way that removes individuals from their own understanding of their bodies and promotes a specific form of knowledge. This can be seen in one way or the need to restrict or abolish sex through abstinence and monogamous practices that exclude condom promotion as a means of HIV prevention; and at an extreme as justification for population control and eugenics.[66] On the other hand this argument is also cited by those who deny the relationship between HIV and AIDS, claiming it to be a form of western knowledge as a form of what Foucault terms the "possibility of resistance" to the "grips of power with the claims of bodies, pleasures and knowledges."[67] Either perspective shows how sex and the body become a biopolitical terrain within the wider framework of global health governance.

The final way in which biopolitics can be applied to understanding global health governance is the relationship between fear and risk. According to Elbe, it is the language of risk that enables biopolitical power to justify, maintain, and extend the power of institutions and sovereign states within global health governance. Risk occupies a central terrain within global health governance in the monitoring of new health threats, surveillance of any new risks within existing diseases and health concerns, and the framing of "risk groups" to be monitored by specific institutions with expertise in monitoring and evaluation.[68] It allows for governance of certain population groups and dynamics, and individuals through biopolitical interventions based on statistical modeling and "targeted" interventions.

Risk is both a social and cultural concept that refers to the potential for harm or worry.[69] The WHO uses risk as part of identifying specific barriers or risks to ill-health. For the WHO, risk refers to "any attribute, characteristic or exposure of an individual that increases the likelihood of developing a disease or injury" and pertains to: tobacco, alcohol, physical inactivity, low fruit and vegetable intake, high cholesterol, high blood pressure, obesity, and high blood sugar.[70] A central operating principle of risk is that of fear. Fear of health risks or disease risks can be used to prompt individuals, communities, and states into action. Globally, pathogenic avian influenza has the ability to prompt fear and thus demand a response in governance innovation due to the, in some cases fatal, threat it poses to humans, despite often having low mortality rates.[71] It is the social amplification of risks by public perception and the media here that is crucial to the formation of reactionary global health governance. It is this social amplification that results in social and economic disruption.[72]

The social and economic aspect to risk perception and its consequences for global health governance are made most obvious by the example of SARS. SARS killed 813 of the 8,427 people infected with it. This is a relatively low number in comparison to other infectious diseases. Conversely the element of fear and risk associated with travel and contamination caused US$54 billion in financial losses.[73] The combination of fear of human suffering, and the wider fear of financial loss compelled a framework of action to be coordinated globally. The need to create new responses to health risks and prioritize specific health concerns is stimulated by risk and the associated impact of fear upon the global political economy. Responding to such risk necessitates reaction by multiple actors and regulations to new threats. This approach to global health suggests its governance has come to constitute a reactive response to risk and the mapping of potential risk.

Conclusion

The approaches to global health governance considered in this chapter suggest the following to our understanding of the subject. The first is that health governance is increasingly less to do with health, than the promotion of human rights, equity, human development, security and biopolitical control. What these approaches have in common is that health interventions are at the core of wider debates within political philosophy: the redistribution of wealth and inequality, individual liberty, and the extension of political power. In each case health is a terrain in which political power is pursued, or is seen as a threat or risk to political stability and individual liberty. Whilst divergent, these approaches to global health suggest its governance is underpinned by problems of the governed and those who govern, who provides, and the outcomes of such provision beyond health benefits. How these approaches manifest in terms of agenda-setting, delivery, and health outcomes is clear when considering specific diseases and illnesses and the institutional structures and initiatives created to respond to them. The next two chapters consider the role of old and new actors in global health governance; their history and structure; and how these approaches to global health manifest themselves in policy and practice.

2 Institutions of global health governance

- The state and bilateral assistance
- Before the WHO: antecedents to global health governance
- World Health Organization
- The UN system
- The World Bank
- International Monetary Fund and the World Trade Organization
- Non-governmental organizations
- Foundations
- Conclusion

At the core of global health governance is a range of intergovernmental organizations, some established to directly address health as part of their core mandate, and others that have come to focus on health as part of a wider effort towards the promotion of international peace, security, and development. The institutionalization of global health has occurred in three waves. The first wave relates to the formation of general rules, norms, and standards developed to govern sanitation and trade-related health concerns and the "golden age" of discovery during the nineteenth century. The second wave marks the consolidation of these norms and standards at the end of the Second World War with the formation of the World Health Organization (WHO) and associated United Nations (UN) specialized agencies working on health provision, as well as the formation of international non-governmental organizations (NGOs) that concentrated on health as a wider part of development and reconstruction. The third wave of institutionalization refers to the rise of partnerships in the early 2000s. The presence, growth, and origins of different actors overlap within these waves, but for the ease of organization this chapter addresses those actors and institutions prominent in global health in the first and second wave, with the presence of new actors as part of the third wave considered in Chapter 3.

This chapter outlines who the main actors in global health are by concentrating primarily on the intergovernmental agencies formed in the early twentieth century, as well as established international non-governmental actors that have formed the framework in which health governance operates. The chapter outlines the growth of global responses to issues of international health by first focusing on the state before exploring how transnational arrangements and regulations around sanitary and trade-related health concerns provided the basis for the League of Nations Health Organization as a precursor to the WHO. The chapter then explores the role of the WHO as the lead agency in global health before considering the associated specialized agencies of the UN for global health—United Nations Children's Fund (UNICEF), United Nations Development Programme (UNDP), United Nations Population Fund (UNFPA); and the role of international financial institutions such as the World Bank, World Trade Organization (WTO) and the International Monetary Fund (IMF). The chapter finishes with an examination of the role of private philanthropy and NGOs in global health governance.

The state and bilateral assistance

The state is the primary site of global health governance. The state provides two important institutional roles within global health governance—the arena in which governing global health takes place and that which provides financial assistance to stimulate global health initiatives either through bilateral or multilateral assistance. This section will consider each of these two roles in turn.

State intervention, whether through minimal public financing and creating incentives or space for private sector support or the provision of social welfare and socialized systems of medicine, has a fundamental role in the governance of global health. Any global intervention made by global intergovernmental agencies, private foundations, or NGOs requires the state to implement and sanction such activities. Whilst in some regards health interventions challenge state sovereignty,[1] the operating principle of all global health initiatives is that they must be sanctioned by the state, sovereignty is paramount, and that government and public support is fundamental to any change in outcome. Without state infrastructure or backing—either by the government or population at large—global health initiatives are seen to fail. However, intrinsic to this is the inclusion of the right kind of state involvement or backing: corrupt or weak states that lack in infrastructure or democratic credentials are said to undermine global health interventions, and in many ways exacerbate global health problems. It is this recognition that has led global health governance to be organized around the principles of good governance: state "ownership," societal or multisectoral "participation," and wider "transparency." The emphasis placed on these principles requires governments to demonstrate successful governance strategies and the allocation of funds to "good" ends. This has specifically been the case within developing countries. Hence, the state comes to have a dual responsibility. It is primarily responsible for the application of global health governance in practice: delivering effective health interventions, outlining strategies in which to do so, and organizing financial support. However, it is also responsible for doing so in a way that promotes the core values of good governance and liberal democracy: transparency, accountability, representation, and participation. Global health governance has thus come to be more than just the promotion of better health for all; it is about doing so in a way that promotes liberal values and democracy in a manner that sustains global health initiatives and rights-based approaches to health.

The second role of the state within global health governance is that of financial assistance and strategic guidance through bilateral and multilateral aid. The core institutions to be discussed in this chapter—the WHO, UN agencies, and the international financial institutions—are all intergovernmental bodies. That is the decisions they make and the core funding they receive on the whole comes from states. State financial support and presence on the governing bodies of these institutions means global health interventions are susceptible to the interests of governments, specifically those that provide the greatest financial assistance and heavier voting rights. Bilateral aid is either given through multilateral institutions or from state to state directly. Bilateral initiatives for global health have grown in relation to increased interest in health and development and a rise in specialized aid agencies. State-based overseas development assistance (ODA) makes up the majority of total spending on global health. Figure 2.1 shows the evolution of total spending on development assistance for health from 1978 to 2007.

As Figure 2.1 shows, total spending on global health stagnated during the 1990s but has continued to grow exponentially since then. Bilateral commitments to global health have reflected this trend. The only change being that in 1978 bilateral assistance was 40 percent of all financing for global health which by 2007 had declined to 37 percent of total financing. State financing is closely matched by NGOs and private financing (to be discussed in more detail below). However, despite a rise in new institutions and private forms of health funding, bilateral assistance remains the dominant model in which health initiatives are financed.

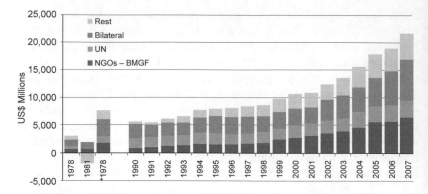

Figure 2.1 Evolution of total development assistance for health to 2007
Note: * Values from WHO Report, 1981, adjusted by inflation.

Bilateral aid takes various forms that often reflect the interests or priorities of the donor. The simplest form of aid is direct to a specific vertical health intervention, from government to government. However, this tends to be the exception in modern global health practice. In practice, direct bilateral aid is given to the government in addition to a host of non-state actors: private companies, community groups, or international NGOs. This aid is either directed by the host donor's aid agency in-country or institutional headquarters or given to general basket funding, where all bilateral aid is pooled within a government agency that is then allocated on the basis of agreement between the state and donor partnership groups. A key concern and problem with the use of bilateral aid in governing global health has been that reflecting the interests and priorities of the donor state makes it deeply political and problematic for wider processes of coordination. Donors may want to fund certain countries and health concerns in a specific manner. This can create multiple health systems and strategies for delivering aid and the sidelining of specific health issues through the prioritization of others. Coordination between bilateral donors becomes difficult. The ability of the recipient state to appropriately strategize and prioritize specific health initiatives then becomes subject to the will of its donor partners.

Key mechanisms of overcoming differences in state priorities and interests are through participation in global fora for decision-making and discussion, and bilateral and multilateral agreements outlining the roles and responsibilities of different states within the international system. States are unable to respond to global health problems alone; they lack the resources, expertise, and monitoring capacity. Global health problems require global responses. Hence agreements, directives, and systems have been established in response to the need of states. The origins of such agreements and systems of governance are to be found in the nineteenth century.

Before the WHO: antecedents to global health governance

Global threats to the health of populations have always existed. The plague, smallpox, cholera, and other diseases spread through poor sanitation and conflict have all had transboundary effects on the health of populations. However, it was not until the rapid industrialization in the nineteenth century that health became a problem that necessitated a coordinated global response. Industrialization and the opening up of new trade routes through the Suez Canal accelerated the spread of health threats through the movement of agricultural goods, people—slaves, seamen, or foreign workers—and increased urbanization and poor, crowded living conditions. One of the most obvious responses to these health threats was the introduction of quarantine; however, excessive measures were seen to limit the growth of trade and thus the wealth and power of dominant states and empires at the time.[2] Instead states engaged in forums to discuss threats to health and the best way of overcoming such threats whilst maintaining economic power and advantage. The two most prominent of such forums was the International Sanitary Conference and the International Conference on Cholera.[3] These conferences reached little agreement and suffered from a lack of biomedical knowledge or expertise on health issues such as tuberculosis, malaria, yellow fever, or cholera. However, they were significant in terms of global health governance in three respects. First, they exemplified the need for global agreement as to the best way to address concerns, and state willingness to engage in multilateral discussion. Second, they reflected the interdependent, complex relationship between trade and global health. Third, the conferences showed that governance without knowledge of specific diseases and health concerns was futile.

The nineteenth century was not only the starting point for global discussions as to how to respond to the threat of ill health and disease, but represented the "golden age" of public health discovery and knowledge. The early part of the century saw the invention of the stethoscope, x-rays, and machines to conduct bacteriological and chemical tests[4] while the second half saw a "revolution" in medical knowledge with the work of scientist Louis Pasteur and medical doctor, Robert Koch.[5] The legacy of Pasteur, Koch and associated researchers of the time such as Edward Jenner and Alexander Fleming, was the discovery and identification of microbes, or germs, as the cause of disease. This breakthrough paved the way for scientific advances in the causes of tuberculosis, anthrax, and smallpox and thus a better understanding of how to prevent, treat, and manage such health concerns.

Understanding the causes and potential responses to diseases facilitated a wider ability to respond and coordinate international standards of hygiene to limit the spread of microbes through the vectors of international trade, seamen, and persons working overseas. At the practice level, doctors in North America and Europe began to put emphasis upon the causes of ill-health through the need for improved water and sanitation and the use of pesticides.[6] Globally, progress in medical research galvanized global support for international coordination, with the establishment of the International Sanitary Regulations in 1903, The Office International d'Hygiene Publique (OIHP), 1907, and the World Congress of International Organizations in 1910.[7] These regulations and institutions presented the first institutionalized form of global health governance and established a number of precedents for its future development.

The emergence of a global health governance framework organized around the International Sanitary Regulations and OIHP became embedded during the interwar period of 1918–39 through the formation of the League of Nations Health Organization in 1920. The League health organization fitted within the overarching ambition of the League of Nations and its architect Woodrow Wilson's commitment to the promotion of peace and security through the right to self-determination and mutual agreements and guarantees between states through international covenants. The principle function of the health organization was to prevent and control disease of international concern and principally focus on the outbreak of diseases such as typhus and influenza following the First World War. The organization was to house the OIHP and International Sanitary Regulations within its over-arching structure and provide a framework for the monitoring and promotion of global health. The organization would extend global health governance beyond disease surveillance and biomedical research to control and prevent new concerns such as cancer and tobacco-related illness. The budget of the organization would be drawn from member states of the League and private philanthropic foundations. This vision of the health organization enshrined the relationship between health and global peace and the involvement of public–private financing that remains pertinent to current expressions of global health governance.

Ultimately like the League of Nations, the health organization failed to launch. The US government at the time resisted the inclusion of the

OIHP within the organization's framework and did not ratify the founding treaty of the League, the Treaty of Versailles. The outbreak of the Second World War led to the collapse of the League and any global cooperation beyond the formation of military alliances. Hence global cooperation towards the provision of better health outcomes, biomedical research into epidemiology and disease control were heavily restricted. What the health organization did, was provide an idea of what a global health institution could look like. Any such health institutions would be made up of a consolidation of the OIHP and International Sanitary Regulations, and reflect the inter-relationships between health, trade, peace, and stability. It is these principles that provide the institutional basis of the WHO.

World Health Organization

The formation of the WHO in 1948 alongside health-related UN agencies such as UNICEF marked a shift towards multilateralism and international organization as a means of addressing global problems in the aftermath of the Second World War. The inception of the WHO fully institutionalized preceding trends in regional health organizing, international regulations, and the need to control and manage infectious disease and emerging pandemics. Underpinning the WHO is the fundamental idea that health is a human right and intrinsic to the personal, social, and economic development of individuals and the states and societies in which they live. Any institution of global health governance would have to be adaptable to changes in the world and the emergence of new health concerns. Health was seen as a common global public good that was not only about the control and regulation of infectious disease but also prioritized chronic and non-communicable diseases such as tobacco-related illness, cancer and cardiovascular disease, and disease eradication.

The WHO has prioritized these concerns through sustained interventions into specific health concerns and diseases and emphasizes the need for primary healthcare provision and the role of health system strengthening. In the first 30 years of its existence the organization focused on a combination of vertical health strategies through efforts towards the eradication of specific diseases such as smallpox, and the horizontal strategies that took primary healthcare as the central operating principle of global health governance. These two methods of intervention were consolidated in the late 1970s with the affirmation of the Alma Ata Declaration and the eradication of smallpox.

In 1978 all member states of the WHO signed the Declaration of Alma Ata. The Declaration committed states to the realization of

"Health for All" through the prioritization and centrality of primary healthcare. The central principles of Alma Ata are:

- health as a state of complete physical, mental, and social well-being is a human right;
- the highest possible level of health is a global social goal involving social, economic, and the health sector that is crucial to social and economic development and world peace;
- inequality between developed and developing countries is unacceptable;
- people have the right to participate individually and collectively in healthcare planning;
- governments have a responsibility to the health of their people and by 2000 all people will have a level of health that allows for a socially and economically productive life;
- socially acceptable methods and technology must be universally accessible to individuals at a cost their communities and countries can afford;
- primary healthcare is characteristic to a specific country; addresses the main health problems of communities; requires non-health interventions in education, agriculture, and nutrition; requires community and individual self-reliance in planning and operation; and relies on local health workers;
- all governments should form national policies and plans to launch and sustain primary healthcare as part of a comprehensive national health system;
- all countries should cooperate in the spirit of partnership; and
- independence, peace, and disarmament "could and should release additional resources" for peaceful aims, of which primary healthcare should receive a significant share.

As the above points suggest, intrinsic to the declaration was a wider recognition and re-assertion of the right to health, and the social, economic, and political drivers of ill-health and the spread of disease. For some, these 10 principles demonstrated the politicization of the WHO, as it explicitly linked global health with wider processes of international politics, political economy, and global transition at the time. However, for others the intention was to not become politicized but to act as more of a function of solidarity among member states of the institution.[8] Regardless of intent, the purpose of Alma Ata was to consolidate member state support for global health and reassert the founding principles of the WHO and hence its central role in global health governance.

The consolidation and reassertion of the role of the WHO during the late 1970s was heightened by the eradication of smallpox by May 1980. Disease eradication as a central strategy for the WHO primarily focused upon two diseases: malaria and smallpox. During the 1950s, the WHO focused its efforts on the importance of epidemiology, parasitology, and entomology as well as advanced scientific techniques and laboratory research.[9] In the context of little progress in the case of malaria, smallpox first came onto the WHO's agenda with Soviet Union backing in 1958,[10] yet it was not until 1966 when the World Health Assembly approved US$2.5 million towards its eradication that the issue fully took hold within the organization.[11]

The WHO's smallpox campaign lasted from 1952 to 1979 with its full eradication being announced on 8 May 1980. This was the first time a disease had ever been eradicated and hence was seen as a triumph for the WHO. The WHO's success showed it could work effectively as a lead agency for health and coordinate research alongside state interests and public–private investment.

The late 1970s and early 1980s marked a significant, galvanizing period for global health governance. The WHO has asserted its role by giving clear direction and leadership in the articulation and fulfillment of specific goals, and primary healthcare as the central priority of global health interventions. This period marked the consolidation of the antecedents to global health that involved multiple public and private actors and research to situate global health as a broader social,

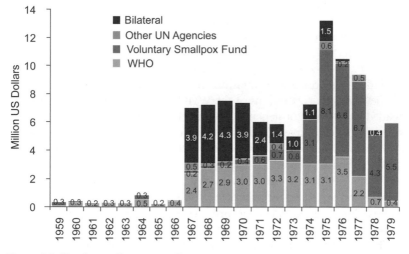

Figure 2.2 Total spending on smallpox

economic, and political concern intrinsically linked with changes in the world, whether political transition, for example, newly independent states or environmental changes. In many ways, however, the WHO has failed to sustain and replicate such success and has faced significant challenges to its leadership and legitimacy.

Structure and organization

The WHO is organized through a combination of member state representation within the World Health Assembly (WHA), expert technical assistance through the executive board, and day-to-day running through the Secretariat overseen by the director-general. The WHO is a three-tiered institution that operates at the global level through its headquarters in Geneva, Switzerland, at the regional level through its six regional offices—African Region, Region of the Americas, South-East Asia Region, European Region, Eastern Mediterranean Region, and Western Pacific Region—and at country level. It is the most decentralized institution within global health governance.

Decision-making and agenda-setting within the WHO occurs through the WHA made up of member states with voting rights, and non-voting observers from NGOs and other international bodies. Decisions within the WHA are made on the basis of one member, one vote, and the principle of agreement by consensus. The WHA meets annually to approve the WHO's work program, annual reports, and budget, and provide overall policy direction to the institution's operations. The executive board is made up of 34 individuals (as of 2007) elected by states on account of their specialized expertise. The purpose of the board is to meet twice a year to advise on constitutional issues, review the WHO's work plan and budget, and advise on emergency measures where necessary. In this sense they provide the technical expertise and overall guidance to member states within the WHA and the wider secretariat.

The day-to-day operations of the WHO are conducted by the secretariat headed by the director-general. The director-general of the WHO is nominated by the executive board and then confirmed by the WHA. The role of the director-general is to oversee the implementation of the WHA and executive board's objectives, and pursue their own vision of the organization through the secretariat's main structures. Activities within the WHO operate through a combination of dialogue and feedback mechanisms within this three-tiered structure, with issue-specific departments in Geneva offering guidance and advice to the regional offices, and vice versa.

The WHO currently identifies its core functions within global health as being: leadership and partnership in health matters, shaping research agendas and disseminating knowledge, standard-setting, monitoring and evaluation, providing technical support and building institutional capacity, monitoring health situations and setting trends, and "articulating ethical and evidence-based policy options."[12] The WHO fulfills these functions through the day-to-day operations of the regional offices and various departments operating in one of the following units: i) Family and Community Health; ii) General Management; iii) Health Action in Crises; iv) Health Systems and Services; v) HIV/AIDS, Tuberculosis, Malaria and Neglected Tropical Diseases; vi) Innovation, Information, Evidence and Research; vii) Health Security and Environment; and viii) Non-communicable Diseases and Maternal Health. The WHO addresses this broad range of health concerns through research and data collection, the dissemination of knowledge, and strong partnerships with member states and international agencies.

Beyond coordination and leadership, the WHO has two important functions within global health governance: standardization and the making and sustaining of international law. Standardization occurs through WHO pre-qualification of medicines and vaccines and the promotion of health systems and outbreak response strategies that ensure global cohesion in the management of health issues. WHO pre-qualification ensures that drugs used throughout the world are safe, effective, and of sufficient quality to use, and reflects the legitimacy of the organization as a technically expertised institution. Standardized responses and outbreak management ensure the containment of emerging threats. A key mechanism of doing so is through the International Health Regulations (IHRs).

The IHRs are a form of international law that binds all member states, other than those who choose to opt out, to report disease outbreaks or emerging health issues to the WHO. They are the consolidation of the International Sanitary Regulations, renamed the International Health Regulations in 1956, with adaptations made in 2005 and brought into effect in 2007.[13] States have to have sufficient core surveillance systems and "response capacities" at every level of the state, with a particular emphasis on international ports and airports and any other potential crossing grounds for disease. The WHO at the regional and country level works with states to assist in developing surveillance and monitoring systems in this regard. In addition to the IHRs, the WHO uses international law as a function of global health governance through conventions such as the Framework Convention on Tobacco Control (FCTC). The 1999 FCTC was the first global health treaty that had a binding resolution on states. By 2008, 160 countries became signatories to the convention, including all G8 states with the exception of the

United States. The key features of the Convention were restrictions on tobacco advertising and sponsorship bans; the introduction of health warnings on tobacco products; a ban on misleading descriptions; an increase in taxation; greater efforts to combat tobacco smuggling; and widespread protection from involuntary exposure.[14] Contentious in its formation and implementation, the convention has had a notable and visible impact on tobacco regulation throughout the world. It has demonstrated that international law is an effective mechanism within global health governance, and that the WHO has the ability and legitimacy to bind states to such agreements and oversee its general enforcement.

The role of international law and standardization provides the WHO with much of its legitimacy and re-enforces its leadership status within global health governance. However, much of this sustained legitimacy and leadership depends on the organization's ability to maintain state compliance with such law and monitor the development of further laws whilst balancing state sovereignty against individual freedoms. It is not necessarily in states' or individuals' interests to report disease outbreaks or to restrict tobacco advertising. In 2003, much media commentary suspected that China was engaged in a "cover up" of the SARS outbreak so as to reduce the impact the disease and its spread would have on China's trade, financial growth, and social cohesion. The US's full involvement with the FCTC has been limited by its domestic interests in tobacco production and consumption. Hence, as with most intergovernmental organizations, the WHO can only make states adhere to international health law through standardized behavior, media pressure, naming and shaming, and framing issues within the national interest.

Challenges

The implementation of international health law by the WHO suggests two key challenges that have underpinned problems within the institution: member state sovereignty and the trumping of economic issues such as trade over global health concerns. The WHO has to balance its fundamental commitment to a right to health against cultural relativism within states and the growing presence of market-based health policies. For Lee, it is this problem between the idealized version of health for all and the practical aspect of doing global health governance or "realpolitik" that has defined the WHO.[15] Compounding such a problem has been wrangling within the institution's internal structure and external challenges to its leadership and impact.

Internally the WHO has suffered from problems with its bureaucracy, leadership, and budgetary constraints. The WHO's budget is made up of a quarter of core member state funding and the rest from voluntary contributions by states, international organizations, and private agencies. This makes budget planning and prioritizing difficult for the institution, as despite making certain projections, its operations are susceptible to this flexible 75 percent. Moreover, as Figure 2.3 shows, whilst the WHO's budget has steadily risen in recent years, it has not done so at such a rapid rate as new institutions.

As Chapter 3 will show, new institutions have been established with expanding budgets and mandates to the detriment of the WHO. This sees a massive skew of financing towards specific diseases and vertical interventions. Hence health for all encompasses of a broad range of health issues and concerns that come into question when financial support is lacking. Whereas the WHO traditionally has been seen as *the* global health institution, its mandate, leadership, and legitimacy are challenged by mission creep of financial institutions such as the World Bank and the budget and vision of new institutions and public–private partnerships. The WHO therefore has to maintain its relevance as the leader in global health knowledge, data, and expertise in how to best address health. In many ways the WHO has struggled to keep up with the wider association of health with development and security concerns, and has maintained a biomedical model of approaching these issues. Whereas many institutions within the UN system have adopted forums for NGO and private sector engagement as standard practice throughout its operations, this is less the case for the WHO. Partnership is integral to its operations, yet such partnerships remain with the

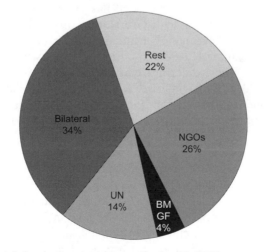

Figure 2.3 Total development assistance for health 2007

Box 2.1 Directors-general of the World Health Organization

Brock Chisholm	1948–53
Marcolino Candau	1953–73
Halfdan Mahler	1973–88
Hiroshi Nakajima	1988–98
Gro Harlem Brundtland	1998–2003
Lee Jong-Wook	2003–6
Margaret Chan	2006–

"old" actors of states and UN agencies. For some, the WHO "has proven inadequate" in responding to new and emerging health threats[16] or maintaining its leadership role among the multiplicity of health actors.

Leadership is vital to the vision and relevance of the institution. Effective directors-general who provide a clear mandate, are forward-thinking, and help the institution adapt to emerging health threats and changes to health systems delivery, are intrinsic to the legitimacy and influence of the WHO. This legitimacy is important for the WHO's authority in global decision-making, relations with member states, and facilitating greater voluntary contributions to the core budget.

As with the heads of most intergovernmental agencies, directors-general tend to be technocratic or charismatic, with their influence dependent on their relationship with the secretariat and member states. As Lee highlights, the director-general has exhibited a number of different styles and attributes, with Gro Harlem Brundtland (1998–2003) being praised as a "visionary," Halfdan Mahler (1973–88) "reified," and Hiroshi Nakajima (1988–98) "criticized" both within and outside the institution.[17] These differing styles of leadership or perceptions of directors-general point to internal discord within the institution that fragments cohesion among the secretariat and regional bodies, and presents an image of institutional bickering and lack of direction to member states and partnering institutions.

The UN system

While the WHO is the lead agency for global health governance within the UN system, multiple UN agencies engage in health-related activities. This has grown specifically over the last 30 years with greater explicit recognition of the linkages between health and development and a focus on the social determinants of *global* health. The result of this has been a much more prominent role for UN agencies such as the UNDP and UNFPA, the creation of specialized agencies out of the WHO such as the Joint United Nations Programme on HIV/AIDS (UNAIDS), and the growth of influence of the international financial institutions, specifically the World Bank. This section will consider the role of three prominent UN agencies relating to global health policy: UNICEF, the UNDP, and UNFPA. Each of these agencies is quite different, but shares similar characteristics in relation to their role in global health governance: they promote rights-based approaches to health, are engaged within wider institutional partnerships, center on reproductive, sexual health, and HIV/AIDS, and with the exception of UNICEF are in part under-funded and lack funding capacity in project implementation.

United Nations Children's Fund

The role of UNICEF within global health governance predates that of the WHO. Formed in 1946 to provide food, clothing, and healthcare for children facing famine and disease in Europe in the aftermath of the Second World War, UNICEF has been a lead institution in governing global health.[18] Initially formed as an ad hoc fund, UNICEF had its mandate extended to become formally institutionalized in 1953. Healthcare and good nutrition are fundamental components of the UN's Declaration of the Rights of the Child that provides the framework for action and compliance for all member states within the UN system.

The inclusion of health within the mandate and operations of UNICEF has adapted within the organization in various ways since its formation. The 1950s–70s saw UNICEF framing health issues as fundamental to child rights: developing state and public support to fund operations, developing recognition of the rights of the child and health, and building trust in UNICEF as a legitimate actor within global health. A key component of this which continues to be at the center of UNICEF's work was immunization. This period saw the foundations of working partnerships between UNICEF and the WHO on issues of child and maternal health. Such partnerships became more institutionalized in the late 1970s–early 1980s with the joint WHO-UNICEF 1979 International Conference on Primary Healthcare and the 1981 International Code of Marketing of Breastmilk Substitutes.[19] These two initiatives show how WHO and UNICEF collaborated closely on support for community-based interventions and standard-setting for states and the private sector. During the 1980s, breastfeeding, oral rehydration, food security, birth spacing, the promotion of growth monitoring, and crucially, immunization, were the overarching objectives of UNICEF.

Immunization and vaccination has been a central activity within UNICEF since its creation. This activity was consolidated in the 1990s as UNICEF and its partners' activities centered upon universal child immunization through better health systems, awareness, community outreach, and social mobilization. Efforts towards universal immunization have been strained by changing investments in child health strategies and divergent and new issues facing child health such as the HIV/AIDS epidemic. Compounding this has been a significant decline or neglect of health systems within developing countries. Immunization strategies saw an increase in relevance and impact in the early 2000s with UNICEF increasing investment in vaccine provision from 7 million in 2004 to 25 million in 2006. This has been part of a wider trend towards emphasizing primary healthcare strategies and health system strengthening, and the achievement of the Millennium Development Goals (MDGs).

The MDGs framed much of the operations of UNICEF during the late 1990s in the build-up to their formation and the agency's operational work thereafter. In 2002 the UN General Assembly revisited the 1990 World Summit for Children to reiterate support and efforts among member states towards better health, nutrition, sanitation, and education for children. Combining the priorities of the MDGs and the General Assembly Special Session, promoting healthy lives, protecting children against abuse, exploitation and violence, and combating HIV/AIDS became the core of UNICEF's operational aims in the 2000s.

UNICEF pursues these over-arching aims through a pattern similar to most UN agencies: increased partnership with states, NGOs, the private sector, UN agencies, and foundations. Community engagement, communication, and participation are a fundamental part of how UNICEF conducts its work. Similar to the majority of UN agencies, UNICEF advocates for the rights and health of the child, and works with states to assist in the development of strategic plans, system strengthening, and monitoring and evaluation. It promotes healthy behavior and practice at the community and household level and engages in evidence-based interventions through conducting its own surveys alongside the state and disseminating information for national strategies. Beyond these core practices, the agency has a direct role in procurement and vaccine delivery. Alongside the UNFPA, UNICEF is one of the largest providers of vaccines for childhood diseases within global health governance.

UNICEF has considerable influence within global health govern-ance. This influence has been extended through its working relationship with WHO and other UN agencies, its presence and trust in donor and partner states, and its ability to secure sustained funding in the provision of vaccines. Comparable to other UN agencies, UNICEF has been able to secure sustained funding from public and private donations. This has made it more resilient and adaptable to changes in member state priorities and enabled it to maintain a clear mandate without having to compromise to the same extent as some other UN agencies. Furthermore, it has positioned itself as an effective brand within global health and global governance more broadly. It has a clear mandate, and despite a plethora of actors working on issues of child health, remains the authority on issues affecting children. The combination of sustained funding, clear mandate, and legitimacy secures the position of UNICEF within global health governance more firmly than other institutions created at the same time such as the WHO.

United Nations Population Fund

The UNFPA was formed as a trust fund within the UN system in 1967 to support and fund population activities within the UNDP. Since 1971, the UNFPA became a standalone agency as a subsidiary organ of the UN General Assembly. The UNFPA is a key actor in global health governance through: i) its partnerships with the UNDP, WHO, and UNICEF; ii) its co-sponsorship of UNAIDS; iii) its rights-based and advocacy role with governments; and iv) its involvement in pro-curement strategies and systems. Through partnership with states and other institutions, the UNFPA is able to ensure the presence of rights-based approaches to health for men, women, boys, and girls. Framed by the Programme of Action agreed by 179 states at the 1994 International Conference on Population and Development, the main principles of the UNFPA's work in health is towards: universal access to reproduc-tive health systems by 2015, a 75 percent decline in maternal mortality by 2015, a decline in infant mortality, increase in life expectancy, and a decline in HIV infection rates.[20] The UNFPA pursues such aims by playing a key advocacy role for issues of maternal and reproductive health and being prominent in the formulation of domestic and global strategic plans. Key to such advocacy is the promotion of gender rights and equal access to health services for men and women and culturally sensitive awareness to how interventions affect people differently.[21] In sum, the UNFPA follows a similar pattern to most UN agencies, in that it provides coherence to reproductive, maternal, and child health interventions, while advocating for their inclusion in state and global health planning strategies.

Beyond advocacy, the UNFPA has a direct role in information and data collection and procurement strategies. The UNFPA works with states in the collection and use of population data in policy planning and future projection initiatives. At the global level, the agency uses such data as part of its wider efforts towards forecasting health security needs and mobilizing and coordinating global support to fulfill such needs. It does so through institutional partnerships, the publication of its annual State of World Population Report, and close working relations with UN member states. The World Population Report and collection of population data are fundamental to the ability of the UNFPA to establish itself as one of the key sources of knowledge for global health. Becoming a source of knowledge translates into go-to power for the institution as it positions itself as a legitimate, leading authority in the areas of population and reproductive health. Such legitimacy is grounded in its UN status as an "honest broker" between states and different international institutions and interactions with in-country partners.

The vital role of the UNFPA within global health is in procurement of health supplies and medicines such as condoms for HIV prevention strategies. This is an often overlooked aspect of global health service delivery, but is a core function of any health system strengthening or vertical intervention. The UNFPA works with multiple bilateral, multilateral, and government agencies, as well as private procurement agents to provide health resources at the right time and in the right place. Procurement involves multiple funding streams, systems of delivery, and a balancing act between what donors are willing to fund and how to plug the gaps that arise from such priorities. In emergency or disaster situations, the UNFPA has an additional role to mobilize resources in support of maternal and child health needs. Hence the UNFPA not only provides resources for the delivery of goods but has an oversight role to help states with procurement planning, and the development of systems to ensure effective and efficient delivery of supplies.

Chapter 5 explores the role of the UNFPA in maternal and child health in more detail. However, this overview suggests the UNFPA presents the following functions within global health governance: knowledge gathering and dissemination on population issues, provision of supplies and services in emergencies, and maintenance of a rights-based advocacy approach to governing health. The role of the UNFPA is thus intrinsic to the realization of the health MDGs and population health more broadly. However, its role and position within global health governance is continuously threatened by claims to population knowledge by institutions such as the World Bank, and an increasingly privatized system of procurement that involved multiple private, public, national, and global actors. Part of its success rests on the ability to make progress in response to the health MDGs and coordinate the multiple actors involved in health service delivery, funding, and advocacy. As a UN agency, the organization has a mediator role within this, but is increasingly being reduced in a crowded space. Part of the problem of UN agencies in this regard is that the emphasis on coordination and knowledge can have the effect of nothing actually being delivered.

United Nations Development Programme

The UNDP has come to the fore of global health governance as the home of the MDGs. Three of the MDGs—Goal 4 Child Health, Goal 5 Maternal Health, and Goal 6 Combat HIV/AIDS and other diseases—concentrate on health issues specifically, with the other five goals having important implications for the impact of disease and the health of different people throughout the world. The role of the UNDP within this is to promote the goals to member states and partner organizations, and as such perform an advocacy function in maintaining their relevance in domestic and global public and private policymaking and project planning. The UNDP acts as a monitor and source of information as to progress within the goals and the performance of institutions within the UN system.[22] Similar to comparable UN agencies working in global health, the UNDP performs an "honest broker" role between states and international donors, supporting states with strategic plans and monitoring systems for measuring MDG outcomes; and maintains partnerships with multiple public, private, global, community, and nationally based actors as a working principle.

The UNDP's explicit role in health beyond the MDGs is in regards to HIV/AIDS as one of its core institutional priorities. The UNDP is technically the lead agency within the UN to concentrate on the governance of HIV/AIDS and how to promote or enhance best practice within the state. As such, the UNDP conducts independent research into the governance of HIV/AIDS, promotes rights-based approaches based on gender equity and sexual diversity, and engages in partnerships through institutional collaborations with the Global Fund to fight AIDS, tuberculosis, and malaria and the co-sponsorship of UNAIDS. Beyond HIV/AIDS, health is only implicit within the UNDP's work on human development and globalization and wider concerns on poverty and well-being. Out of 19 of the UNDP's flagship Human Development Reports, none have taken global health or a specific health issue as the standalone basis for the Report. Health has been an intrinsic element to other Reports such as, 2009 Human Mobility and Development, 2007/7 Fighting Climate Change, 2006 Beyond Scarcity, and 2005 MDGs, but has never had a prominent role within this high-profile publication.

The role of the UNDP within global health governance is thus the promotion of the right sort of democratic, accountable governance within HIV/AIDS interventions, and the management of the MDGs. Chapters 4 and 5 consider the role of the health MDGs in more detail, and it is important to suggest here that their role in shaping global health interventions is intrinsic to understanding changes in global health governance in the early 2000s, hence the UNDP is influential in global health by association. The UNDP explicitly links health concerns with wider processes of governance reform. However, the role of the UNDP in the promotion of economic and social development and the linkages between health, poverty, and development have been supplanted by other actors within the global system with bigger budgets and a wider source of in-house expertise, most notably the World Bank.

The World Bank

Since its creation in 1944 as part of the Bretton Woods Institutions, the World Bank has become a prime actor in global health governance. Established to reconstruct Europe after the Second World War, the bank's mandate has expanded from reconstruction to poverty and development, situating health as core within this. The role of the bank in global health really came to the fore in the 1970s with the appointment of Robert McNamara (1968–81) who shifted the bank's approach and policy-lending profile towards a more holistic approach to development that addresses the social determinants of poverty. McNamara outlined his vision for the bank's role in global health in his 1971 address to the board of governors at the bank's September annual meetings, highlighting the problem of nutrition as a central obstacle to development.[23] The bank's first policy-lending to health concerns was a country-specific family planning loan of US$2 million to Jamaica. Its second, disease-specific initiative was in 1974 for an onchocerciasis (river blindness) Control Program in West Africa. More broad-based health sector policies were not approved by the bank until 1979.

The bank's role in health policy has grown exponentially since the inception of the Population Project Department in 1969.[24] However, it was not until the 1980s that the bank became directly linked with healthcare through its co-financing of health sector programs, and indirectly through the socio-economic impact of structural adjustment, and neoliberal reform in partnership with the IMF. The relationship between decline in health provision, structural adjustment, and debt has occupied the majority of understanding of the bank in global health. Structural adjustment policies are a form of conditional-based lending, in which states receiving funds from the bank for a particular project or a loan from the IMF have to adhere to specific policy recommendations towards privatization of state services. Key to this is the reduction of state intervention, the rule of market economism, and conditionality within health sector reform.[25] These policies led to the reduction of healthcare provision through a decline in hospital expenditure and staffing, the introduction of service user fees to be paid by the individual, and responsibility shifting away from the state to the individual.[26] The impact of these policies was most acutely felt within developing countries.

Perhaps the clearest outline of the bank's approach to global health during this time was its 1993 World Development Report *Investing in Health* (WDR 1993). WDR 1993 was interpreted as a means of embedding the bank's market-driven approach to welfare. It articulated the need for privatized healthcare, widespread use of user fees, minimal state interference, and the role of the market.[27] Using health as the focus of the bank's flagship publication makes a clear statement of both the bank's role at the center of global health, and its commitment to privatized forms of healthcare in developing countries. According to Buse and Gwin, the decline of health provision through state welfare, the introduction of new forms of co-financing and user fees by the bank allowed it to make claims to knowledge and expertise in health reform,[28] and consolidate its role as a central actor within global health.[29]

External criticisms of structural adjustment and internal bank reviews as to the effectiveness of its health policies have led to a slight adjustment to the economic liberal values underpinning its health interventions during the late 1980s and early 1990s. Simply put, health services had not improved, and in some countries were in decline. The Bank's explanation for this was that it had not taken account of the systemic conditions or infrastructure needed for improvement. This recognition combined with wider reform packages occurring within the bank during the late 1990s[30] led to a refocus of the institution's global health policies towards systemic reform as to the role of the state and privatized provision, targeted interventions, and most notably a "sector-wide" approach.[31] As Chapter 2 outlined, this sector-wide approach referred to the need to involve all aspects of the public and private sectors and the individual in the provision of healthcare. Central to this change in the direction of the bank was the director of health, nutrition, and population, Richard Feachem (1995–99), who according to a series of articles by Kamran Abbasi in the *British Medical Journal*, focused attention away from user fees and structural adjustment and towards issues of sustainability and working relations with other international actors such as the WHO.[32]

Since 1997 and the introduction of the Comprehensive Development Framework/Poverty Reduction Strategy Paper approach to lending the World Bank has attempted to distance itself from the negative connotations of structural adjustment for health. It has done so by promoting a "good governance" agenda that facilitates partnership and dialogue between the bank and its partner state and non-state actors. The aim is to promote participation, accountability, and transparency within borrower states as key mechanisms of good governance. As such, the bank presents the image of moving away from the "top-down" "hard" politics that have come to characterize the work of the WTO and IMF by promoting a holistic "bottom up" approach to development. This approach has acutely been felt within healthcare where the bank has developed its commitment to forms of community engagement, health system reform, and sector-wide planning. The bank's approach to health as a global public good situated within its holistic approach to development is only one explanation as to why it engages with health policy. An alternative explanation would be the role of health in maintaining the bank's position as a leader in development knowledge and expertise. In positioning itself at the heart of global health policy, the bank presents alternative approaches to public health that break from the norm of public health interventions. These alternatives fulfill the international community's desire for new, innovative solutions to global health, whilst consolidating the bank's position at the center of development knowledge and expertise, and thus its wider relevance to global politics.

The bank has developed and expanded its role in global health through increased and new forms of financing and flagship projects. According to data from the bank's Health Nutrition and Population sector; total health financing peaked at US$2.4 billion in 1996, and maintained a median average of US$1.4 billion between 1997 and 2007.[33] Pertinent to understanding the role of the bank within global health is not the quantity of finance, but the type of financing and how it develops models of best practice. Over the last 10 years the bank has developed these models through its "soft" approach to conditional lending as part of its wider good governance strategy prioritizes government "ownership," community "participation," a "sector-wide" approach to health, and new forms of lending. In health terms, this has translated into the following types of programs and directives.

The first shift in approach has been the bank's relationship with borrower states and a focus away from purely health aspects of government. The bank's holistic, sector-wide approach to global health has seen a prioritization of multiple aspects of government systems within developing countries, grouped together under an umbrella coordinating agency located at the center of government. The second shift in the bank's approach to global health has been community provision. As a wealth of research into global public health interventions would suggest, community participation and inclusion in delivery of health services is not a new phenomenon. However, the bank has developed processes of community inclusion through new forms of community financing. As part of its community-driven development approach, the bank has directed unprecedented funds to non-state actors, specifically grassroots community groups. It has done so through the formation of local state structures designed to identify, fund, and monitor community activity, and through making funds available to loose-knit organizations without any stringent conditions or guidelines. The role of women here is of particular relevance. As previously outlined, part of the role of healthcare within the bank's wider economism agenda is the health of reproducers, producers, and consumers within the global economy. Women form a specific function within this as they are not only integral to reproduction, but provide the care, support, and upbringing of consumers and producers within the global economy. Social protection funds not only address the core of health provision and ensure healthy workers and consumers, but expand the market by bringing women into its logic through lending, competition, and efficiency. Social protection thus reflects the workings of the bank's liberal economist logic at the most personal level of international intervention: the family and the individual. The third change in the bank's global health strategy has been the emphasis placed on sector-wide, multisectoral approaches to health. This approach is evident in the bank's emphasis upon the involvement of the non-health sector within the national governance of health issues and in the level of community involvement within these initiatives.

The above examples of state ownership, community participation, and multisectoral collaboration present the image of a collaborative bank that whilst maintaining a level of conditionality is much more friendly-faced than structural adjustment reform. The bank's economist, conditional-lending, liberal emphasis remains; but whereas these issues were presented as problems in the past, the "good governance" incarnation of the bank's work is presented by the bank as more adaptable to the needs of states in their ability to respond to global health concerns. The World Bank is an important actor in global health because of the indirect impact of structural reform on health systems, the promotion of good governance in the delivery of better health outcomes, and its role in funding high-profile health projects. The bank differs from UN agencies in this regard, as it has the budget and mandate to finance projects and carry out health interventions in partnership with states. It is thus able to transcend a coordination role to influence decision-making through a financial incentive. These roles are important, but often not evident on first examination of health systems and interventions as the bank promotes a benevolent supporting role. The bank is not benevolent but an ever-present actor in global health.

International Monetary Fund and the World Trade Organization

In addition to the World Bank, the two other Bretton Woods Institutions— the IMF and the WTO play an indirect yet vitally important role in the governance of health. Neither the WTO nor IMF have health-specific projects that they fund, or health sectors of their organizations; however, their policies and decisions are of direct relevance as to how health is governed. Similar to the World Bank, the IMF's role in governing health has predominantly been understood in relation to the impact of structural adjustment programs on healthcare reform in developing countries, and the wider introduction of privatization as a global phenomenon in the development and management of public health systems during the 1980s. As the previous section highlighted, IMF loans to developing countries were conditional on a country restructuring its economy to be more open to global trade and financial flows, reducing state intervention in managing the economy, and reforming the banking and public sector to stimulate private partnerships and investment. The net effect on health was a decline in spending on health system strengthening in developing countries because funds were squeezed elsewhere, the introduction of user fees to public health services, and the promotion of subcontracting to private firms and businesses. The logic was that a reduced role for the public sector would leave space for private investment that is more cost-effective, expertised, and efficient to grow and fill this gap. This would make delivery of health services much more effective. However, evidence would suggest this did not happen, but instead led to sustained under-funding of health systems; lack of access for those living in poverty, particularly in rural areas;

migration of health professionals to better paid positions abroad; and a decline in the consumption of drugs as costs increased.[34]

The role of privatization and reduction of state provision of healthcare is not just relevant to the structural adjustment policies of the IMF during the 1980s. The approach the IMF takes to public sector reform is much the same; it is just the mechanisms of implementation that have changed. The IMF now places more emphasis on state inclusion in the reform process and the need to address the shortcomings of global governance in managing global financial affairs. For governing global health, this first means that states, particularly those of developing countries, are given a stake in the process and are thus seen as more likely to implement these reforms. Second, it means that the emphasis on the private sector as the best means of promoting health for all remains the paradigm in which the IMF, and thus those states that borrow from it, operate within. For the IMF, it is not privatization or the private sector's involvement in global health that led to a decline in health system funding; it was the inability of states to implement the reforms properly in addition to the emergence of new diseases such as AIDS and the resurgence of malaria and tuberculosis. The solution to this problem is thus not a decline in the role of the private sector, but the development of the state in developing countries to support its wider investment.

The WTO's role in the governance of health is far less prescriptive in this regard yet has considerable influence over the management and deployment of resources in achieving better health for all. As the antecedents to global health governance have shown, trade and health have always been intrinsically linked through the spread and growth of both. The overarching purpose of the WTO was initially envisioned in the precursor to the organization—the General Agreement on Tariffs and Trade (GATT)—as the liberalization of world trade through the free flow of goods *and,* following on from the Uruguay Round of trade negotiations, services. Through its ministerial and general councils, the WTO manages trade disputes, monitors global trade, provides a forum for negotiation and reviews and assists in national trade policies. Health is on the agenda of the WTO in four ways: i) the health of working populations; ii) migration; iii) trade-related intellectual property rights (TRIPs); and iv) the trumping of trade liberalization over health concerns.

WTO efforts to oversee and facilitate the expansion of global trade mean that workers are more transitory and production more dispersed. Mobile capital and trade flows mean investment opportunities and production sites are not just located in an individual company's home country, but can be based in a variety of locations in which labor is cheap and flexible and supported by minimal state intervention or regulation. The extreme result of this can lead to a race to the bottom in terms of labor standards as companies invest in production sites where worker rights and conditions are restricted. These conditions can affect the respiratory and sanitary health of workers, as well as leading to muscular and joint problems from repetitive labor without breaks. Hence trade liberalization of goods without clear labor standards that enshrine the health and well-being of workers is often detrimental to wider efforts to promote health for all.

The relationship between labor and health extends to the movement of people, particularly skilled workers, in selling their services abroad. This has had a direct impact on health systems in developing countries as trained health professionals leave under-funded health systems to seek better opportunities abroad. This has two impacts on the health of a population. In the first instance it can help improve the health of a population as the supply and expertise of health professionals become more globalized and there is an incentive to create supply to meet the demand. The result of this is that you have areas that specialize in the production and exportation of health professionals such as the Philippines that trains a surplus of nurses to work in-country and abroad. This has proved an effective model for the Philippine economy as health workers send back money to their families in remittances. The second impact of the globalization of services, however, has been the "brain-drain" effect of skilled migrants leaving countries with a high level of demand for their services, as seen in sub-Saharan Africa, particularly in Zimbabwe.

One of the most contentious aspects of the WTO's role in health is that of the protection and enforcement of trade-related intellectual property rights, or the TRIPs agreement. TRIPs have become contentious within global health governance because of their impact on the provision and cost of drugs under patent. TRIPs promote the right to health by ensuring investment, innovation, and research into new and better medicines. Without protection and an ensured return on their investment pharmaceutical companies would have less incentive to invest in research and development for particular drugs and thus these drugs and much-needed medicines would not exist. However, the corollary argument to this is that TRIPs prevent those that need medicines from accessing them as patents make the cost of drugs disproportionately high in countries where the need and rate of return is the highest. Patent protection on specific drugs varies, but at a minimum is set at 20 years. Once a drug is off-patent, it can be reproduced by other companies at a lower cost for the consumer.

The complex and emotive response to the TRIPs when applied to the development of new drugs for tuberculosis or antiretroviral treatment for HIV/AIDS has forced the WTO to publicly acknowledge its role within the governance of health in response to public health emergencies. As part of the 2001 Doha Declaration the WTO acknowledged the right to health of all its member states and flexibility within this. States would be given a degree of flexibility in deciding whether specific health concerns constitute a case for compulsory licensing for export.[35] As such, the introduction of parallel importing and compulsory licensing of drug patents allowed for flexibility within the TRIPs agreement, but there remains a lack of symmetry between the cost of research, development, and production of certain drugs and their purchasing cost. In cases where these flexibilities have been deployed, groups of powerful developed states often join to buffer their use within the WTO.[36] By 2003, the WTO's general council addressed the problem of developing country access through the Implementation of Paragraph 6 of the TRIPs Agreement and Public Health that aimed to address the grey area of access to medicines in developing countries, particularly for pertinent diseases such as HIV/AIDS. However, this grey area remains blurry, and flexibilities are subject to the influence of key states keen to protect the investment of their national companies. Most pharmaceutical companies are based in the global north, with emerging markets in Brazil and India, and little to no presence within low income or less developed countries within the WTO.[37] As Chapter 3 shows, initiatives to stimulate investment in research and development and meeting the requirements of both pharmaceutical companies and developing countries has seen the emergence of public–private partnership models to guarantee the return on investment into specific drugs.

The WTO's acknowledgment that the provision of public health does have a role within its decisions and operating structures suggests some flexibility and accommodation of health concerns. However, beyond the small amendments to the TRIPs agreement there is little evidence of this. As Bloche and Jungman have highlighted, WTO decisions on food safety, asbestos, mad cow disease, and tobacco have "produced bitter conflicts" within the WTO's dispute settlement mechanism.[38] A key example of this has been tobacco. As the above section on the WHO outlined, the FCTC is a binding treaty that regulates the advertising, promotion, and smuggling of tobacco. However, in restricting the flow of tobacco-based products and the promotion and transnational appeal of tobacco, the FCTC arguably provides a barrier to free trade. This argument has often been put forward by large tobacco companies and supportive politicians as a means to circumvent the restrictions of the convention. The WTO has not had a clear role in this debate, but the potential for contentions between health and trade objectives is pertinent.

These concerns suggest that the promotion of health for all and liberalization of world trade can at times seem like contradictory aims. The WTO is fundamentally an organization that provides a forum for states to discuss issues pertaining to the expansion and maintenance of trade liberalization; thus to an extent it has no role or mandate to promote better health outcomes for all. Efforts to address such contradictions may rest in greater inclusion of health issues on the formal agenda of the WTO either through direct representation of the WHO within the institution's general council or wider recognition and advocacy on the part of better health for all through a more balanced trade system for developing countries. These efforts depend, however, on voting cleavages between states and the construction of political will that recognizes health as intrinsic to the full liberalization of world trade and therefore as of equal value. As the case of TRIPs demonstrates, when issues of global health come up on the WTO's agenda, the general tendency of the ministerial and general councils is to defer responsibility and decision-making to the state.

Non-governmental organizations

Provision of healthcare has always extended beyond the state to include individual responsibility and social arrangements among friends and family to provide better health outcomes where they live. In this sense, provision of health services by non-state actors has preceded the role of the state. International NGOs such as Save the Children engaged in health activities before the WHO was even established. The intrinsic relationship between health and development has seen different health strategies—from water and rural sanitation projects to high-level malaria campaigns—consistently prominent on the agenda of NGOs. The number and scope of NGOs active within global health provision increased significantly during the 1980s as state financing of health services declined. During this period NGOs filled gaps left by the state, private sector and international institutions in providing multiple types of service delivery. As NGOs provided health services, their expertise and utility in turn became more widely recognized by states and international donors. For many international donors, NGOs are seen to have greater capacity, trustworthiness, and infrastructural access to local communities than the state in developing countries. For developing countries, NGOs have potential advantages in regards to their reach, expertise, and advocacy; however, in some countries this relationship can be uneasy as NGOs could be viewed as a threat to the government of the time or somehow distorting financial support away from the state. These views have in various guises translated into working partnerships between the state and international donors, and a shift in the role of NGOs from advocacy and service delivery interventions to decision-making and agenda-setting. As such, NGOs at the national, regional, or international level have become the most institutionalized form of non-state health provision and perform several important functions within global health governance.

The legitimacy of NGOs principally derives from their proven track record on service delivery. Historically, the key role NGOs play in service delivery for better health outcomes has been the provision of medical services in emergency or conflict situations. Organizations such as the International Committee of the Red Cross (ICRC) predate the formation of most institutions of global health governance. Established by Swiss businessman Henry Dunant in 1859, the purpose of the ICRC was to provide medical relief for wounded soldiers and civilians, irrespective of their cause or army.[39] Based on the 1949 Geneva Convention, the ICRC acts as a politically neutral humanitarian organization that provides protection and assistance to "victims of war and armed conflict."[40] The organization only operates in countries with the formal acceptance of the state, and has worldwide recognition as a neutral humanitarian body. In addition to the ICRC, organizations such as Médecins Sans Frontières are fundamental to the delivery of healthcare in emergency and conflict situations. They are internationally recognized and maintain the non-political nature of health and the provision of medical treatment.

Though emergency and conflict-based interventions are a considerable element of NGO work on global health, the majority of their work in service delivery takes place in non-conflict situations. NGOs engage in a variety of health activities: from funding medical centers, behavior change communication, procurement and distribution of bed nets for malaria, provision of clean water, to the training of health professionals. In the majority of developing countries, NGOs have become the central partners of states in implementing health-specific strategic plans and reaching measurable targets, and in some areas supplant the role of the state in terms of coordination and delivery. NGOs are generally seen as having closer links with local communities and wider infrastructure than the state in some respects in getting resources and services to the most people. As such, they have become a key component of donor aid strategies, and are involved in meetings with local and national government structures in deciding specific priorities and how such priorities will be met.

Service delivery does not exist to the exemption of more traditional NGO roles in advocacy campaigns. NGOs advocate on the part of specific health issues, regional problems, and the need to maintain a rights-based approach to health for all. Advocacy takes the form of global campaigns to highlight and change public opinion to specific issues, direct lobbying of government agencies, donor countries and intergovernmental organizations, and global media campaigns, often in support of funding drives. Since the 1990s, forms of direct NGO engagement have become an institutionalized principle of agencies such as the World Bank and UNDP. These agencies previously engaged with NGOs on more of an ad hoc basis, but now involve them in project planning strategies, have quotas of NGO involvement in their in-country projects, and ensure presence at events such as the WHA. As such, NGOs have played a fundamental part in getting specific issues on the table. A key example of this has been the transnational activism surrounding HIV/AIDS, which was transformed from a stigmatized "African" or "gay" issue into a global problem that required a global response. For some working in health, NGOs were vital for "going loud" on issues such as HIV/AIDS when governments were not forthcoming.[41] In other instances and for other diseases where an organized advocacy campaign or issues-based group is lacking, the specific health issues have been sidelined and neglected.[42] The success of advocacy strategies often depends on the issue, how it is framed, the network between groups in the global north and south, and the degree to which the campaign has access to decision-making or space for inclusion within an institution.

The scale of NGO involvement in global health has led to greater scrutiny as to the legitimacy and transparency of their involvement. NGOs working on global health issues tend to originate from northern, western states whilst carrying out their central activities in developing countries within the south. This raises questions over the degree to which they are able to speak for those they work with and their understanding of the political system. Their presence in state and intergovernmental bodies can be seen as distorting attention away from less powerful states within the international system. For example, institutions such as the ICRC have a greater presence within the meetings of the WHO than governments from small developing countries. Part of their presence is because of their expertise, but this distortion questions the intergovernmental character of the WHO. In-country their involvement in service provision has supplanted the role of the state in providing basic needs and services for its citizens. Whilst NGOs are able to provide infrastructure where it is lacking within the formal apparatus of the state, their involvement may offset any impetus on the state taking responsibility for this role. A key mechanism of overcoming this has been the joint collaboration between the state and NGOs, working in partnership in the delivery of key services. However, as NGOs become more involved in fulfilling what is seen as traditionally governmental roles and occupying a seat within government decision-making bodies their non-governmental and non-political nature comes to be questioned.

The non-governmental and non-political nature of NGOs is often questioned in regards to where and how they direct their resources, and those issues they advocate on behalf of. Similar to most institutions of global health, NGOs are dependent on the financial resources that support their activities and therefore have to use those health concerns that appeal to the most private donations. For example, infant mortality is an issue that elicits widespread public concern and thus donations, whereas neglected tropical diseases are harder to sell. NGOs are thus involved in the political decision of what is on the global health agenda and what is not. Neutrality of NGOs working in crisis or conflict situations is often questioned by states or used by states as a means of undermining their activities. For example, during the conflict in Afghanistan (2001–) the ICRC was framed in a negative light by the Western media for giving medical assistance to the Taliban despite the army personnel being aware of their activities and understanding of the right of all wounded to healthcare regardless of who they were.[43] Neutrality of NGOs engaging in health activities thus becomes a source of political debate and contention.

A final implication NGO activity has for global health governance is that of confusion and the marketized nature of their activities. The increased number of NGOs and funding for specific diseases has led to a form of market where different types of NGO—those with longevity in the field or newly emerged "briefcase NGOs"[44]—compete within a market of donor aid. This competition and growth of actors leads to confusion and a lack of coordination among global health actors. A key component to address such confusion has been the promotion of multisectoralism, where all actors within the state—non-state, govern-mental, and private—interact in the delivery of health services within a commonly agreed upon strategy for action. Multisectorality is beneficial to health governance as it encourages participation and attention to health concerns; however, it can also lead to wider confusion among multiple actors and parties and distort accountability structures.

Foundations

Private philanthropic foundations have been at the cornerstone of funding and shaping global health governance since the "golden age" of the late eighteenth century. This period saw the growth in private philanthropy, with an increased role for foundations such as the Milbank Memorial Fund, Sage Foundation and Commonwealth Fund in global health governance.[45] Philanthropy became involved with global health governance at this time through the funding of multilateral initiatives such as the Rockefeller Foundation supporting over a third of the League of Nations' Health Organization's budget,[46] and funding of research centers in public health such as the establishment of the Johns Hopkins School of Hygiene and Public Health in 1916 by a joint initiative between the Rockefeller Foundation and the International Health Board.[47] The growth of research centers during this time galvanized the progress of the golden era to focus on areas of health research that developed the biomedical aspect to include emerging health concerns such as tobacco-related disease[48] and saw increased focus on the science of epidemiology—the study of the incidence and distribution of disease, and of its control and prevention.

The pattern remains that foundations support global health initiatives through funding of specific health interventions, investment in research, development and education, and collaborating with public bodies towards the promotion of health for all. Different foundations invest in health for a variety of reasons, yet generally can be seen as a result of personal compulsion, religious belief, tax avoidance, an interest in or retirement from political office, or the pursuit of medical knowledge. They are often met with positive public approval and trust yet remain mainly unaccountable to those they support or the investments they make beyond their board of trustees, or as is often the case, family members. The majority have not undertaken "serious or sustained evaluation" of their work.[49] There has been a considerable rise in the number and scope of philanthropic foundations from 1990 onwards, specifically in regard to high-profile diseases such as HIV/AIDS. This section considers the role of three influential foundations in governing global health: the Rockefeller Foundation, the Ford Foundation, and the Bill and Melinda Gates Foundation.

The Rockefeller Foundation

John D. Rockefeller has defined modern understandings of private philanthropy and global health strategies derived from private wealth.

Having accumulated substantial private wealth through oil refinery, according to Kiger, Rockefeller believed "the power to make money is a gift from God ... to be developed and used to the best ability for the good of mankind" hence he identified making money to serve all as his "duty."[50] For Rockefeller, the best way of serving mankind was through greater research into health, specifically global health. He developed this interest first through the establishment of The Rockefeller Institute for Medical Research in 1901 and the Rockefeller University Hospital in 1910, which continues today as the Rockefeller University for biomedical research; and the Rockefeller Sanitary Commission (1910–14) focusing on multiple health concerns, specifically hookworm in the southern states of the United States.[51] Rockefeller established a precedent in becoming the first US philanthropic organization to obtain a federal charter to work abroad. Attempts to secure government approval failed on the first three applications to the US Congress; however, in 1913 Rockefeller created the International Health Commission within the Foundation as a means of addressing global health concerns[52] and "the well being of humanity around the world."[53] By 1928, the Foundation's total assets amounted to US$200 million. Similar to most philanthropic foundations for health, these assets were overseen directly by Rockefeller and his close confidant and Baptist minister Frederick T. Gates. Since Rockefeller's death the trusteeship of the organization has been with the Rockefeller family, who have a direct role in the Foundation's management alongside its president.

The Rockefeller Foundation had the following implications for global health. It was the first philanthropic organization to develop a global health program with the underlying logic of health for all that would be adopted by the League of Nations and the WHO. Rockefeller gave US$600 million to philanthropic causes in his lifetime.[54] The foundation existed before the formation of formal intergovernmental bodies and in many ways provided the framework for understanding that health mattered, global interventions were possible, and private finance would be a key component within this. It established a precedent for private wealth to be used to better global health outcomes and that this process would be directly overseen by the founder of the organization, with management and trusteeship falling directly to family and close acquaintances. Moreover, the operations of the foundation— from economic development in West Africa in the 1980s, to sustainable use of resources in the 1990s, to the Foundation's current portfolio to manage health and environmental change through "Smart Globalization" that focuses on health system strengthening, surveillance and "impact investing" in the poor[55]—signals the Foundation as having clear presence and permanence in the management of global health and efforts to promote better health. In so doing, however, it also raises the questions of accountability, representation, and transparency in decision-making familiar to private enterprise. Decision-making and agenda-setting continues to be established by the foundation's trustees and management structures in the US. While the foundation has regional bases across the world, as a grant-making facility, agendas and structures remain highly centralized.

The Ford Foundation

The Ford Foundation established by Henry Ford provides a different model of philanthropy to that of the Rockefeller Foundation. According to Kiger, unlike Rockefeller, Ford made no claim to be compelled to philanthropy through a religious compulsion to make money to help people, but engaged in philanthropic work later on in life, for some in response to President Roosevelt's high income and inheritance tax laws of 1935 and the high number of requests Ford received per year asking for money.[56] Ford established the Ford Foundation in 1936 with a basis of $25,000 which was to grow to $37.5 million over his lifetime.[57] The purpose of the foundation was "advancing human welfare" through several of Ford's personal interests. Health was thus one constituent element of many. In its current guise, the Ford Foundation is involved in global health as part of its wider activities on democratic accountability, economic fairness, scholarships, freedom of expression, human rights, housing, social justice, and sustainability. The foundation's interventions in health differ from the Rockefeller approach to health system strengthening, surveillance, and biomedical research, to focus more specifically on interventions into sexual and reproductive health rights through education, research, and the promotion of the right to health.

The Ford Foundation has had a prominent but less of a large impact on the governance of global health. However, it demonstrates an important model for alternative ways of thinking about philanthropy and health governance. First, not all philanthropy is driven by some moral good or religious fervor but can be linked to responding to need or to avoid heavy tax levies. Second, interventions into health through private philanthropy are often part of wider strategies by a foundation. Health for the Ford Foundation is intrinsically linked to rights-based approaches that emphasize democratic accountability and reform promoted by the organization. Finally, philanthropic bodies have been interested in both research and health system strengthening and monitoring and vertical interventions into disease-specific issues. Bringing together key features from both the Rockefeller and Ford Foundations is the Bill and Melinda Gates Foundation.

The Bill and Melinda Gates Foundation

The Bill and Melinda Gates Foundation (hereafter Gates Foundation) was established by the founder of Microsoft Bill Gates and his wife Melinda Gates in 2000. The purpose of the foundation was to merge the interests of two existing philanthropic endeavors by the Gates family—the William H. Gates Foundation and the Gates Learning Foundation—into one as a means of promoting global health, education, and public libraries, and support for families living in Washington and Oregon. Both Bill and Melinda Gates were "shocked by the neglect particularly in terms of research and innovation around diseases that affect people in poor countries"[58] and as such developed a personal interest in the development and delivery of new technologies. The foundation is a grant-making body with an endowment of US $36.4 billion that emphasizes new technologies, innovations, and research into combating some of the world's biggest health problems through its Global Health Program. Since its establishment, the foundation has been described by *The Lancet* as having "changed the landscape for the global-health research community"[59] in that it is the biggest source of private development assistance for health and has an annual budget more than that of the WHO.[60]

As Figure 2.4 shows, in 2010 the Gates Foundation provided 7 percent of total development assistance for health. This money goes to a variety of initiatives. Initially the foundation concentrated on vertical interventions into specific diseases, but has become more involved in processes of health system strengthening. The Global Health Program engages in disease-specific initiatives through vaccine research, broader studies into disease prevention and detection technologies, scaled up community interventions, and institutional, state, and private partnerships or what the Foundation calls "Discovery, Delivery, Policy and Advocacy."[61] The foundation tackles a broad range of health issues: HIV/AIDS, malaria, tuberculosis, pneumonia, neglected disease, enteric and diarrheal diseases, family planning, tobacco control, maternal, neonatal and child health, nutrition, and vaccine preventable diseases.[62] A key strategy within the foundation is disease eradication, specifically through vaccination.

As of 2010, the Foundation had spent US$4.5 billion on vaccine research and had committed a further US$10 billion.[63] The key targets for vaccine research are malaria, guinea worm, HIV, and specifically

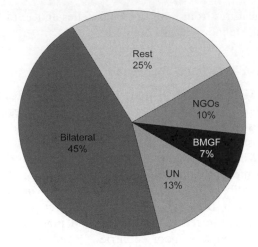

Figure 2.4 Total development assistance for health 2010

polio. Polio eradication has become one of the overarching aims of the Foundation. A core feature of the Foundation has been its ability to invest heavily into research as a means of gaining a greater reward with less immediate results in return for the Foundation's investment. Beyond vaccine research, a defining feature of the Foundation's work in global health has been the scaling up of successful interventions through standard intervention packages and the promotion of efficient and sustainable results-based strategies as the defining mechanism of global health governance. For the Foundation, the Global Health Program (with the exception of vaccine research) is all about funding successful projects that show results quickly and then replicating them rapidly among a wide range of actors and processes.

In addition to funding various projects and research into better global health outcomes, the foundation extends its influence within global health governance through partnerships. The foundation funds intergovernmental organizations such as the World Bank, and is the biggest single donor to WHO; giving grants towards the health metrics network, polio eradication, to strengthen scale-up of maternal, neonatal, and child health interventions[64] and scale up procurement and production of HIV/AIDS, tuberculosis, and malaria drugs. The foundation is one of the largest funders of GAVI (discussed in more detail in Chapter 3) and the Global Fund, and has board presence on the organizations it funds. As one representative of the foundation suggests, "it would certainly be odd for us not to go to the World Health

Assembly."[65] It has a clear presence (but not with voting rights) within decision-making fora such as the WHA, and the "Health 8" (see Chapter 3). The lack of voting rights does not restrict the foundation's impact on decision-making within the WHA: its research budget makes it a leader in global health knowledge, it has large lobbying potential, and the gravitas of Bill Gates affords the foundation a greater degree of access to state leaders, UN workers, media attention, and public opinion.

Organizationally, the Foundation is funded by the Gates Family, Warren Buffet and private contributions, and run by the Gates Family and ex-Microsoft executives. The three co-chairs of the foundation are Bill, Melinda and William Gates Sr, with ex-Microsoft Business Division President Jeff Raikes as the Foundation's chief executive officer. Geographically, the Foundation gives grants to countries across north and south America, sub-Saharan Africa, Europe, India, China, and Australia, as well as having country offices in Seattle, Washington, London, New Delhi, and Beijing. Decision-making however rests in Seattle. The Global Health Program has individual strategies based on specific diseases or health issues that are developed and managed from the central Seattle office. Implementation is then conducted by grant recipients and those organizations funded by the foundation. It is these organizational structures and the influence of the foundation within global institutions that has led to some of its criticism.

For observers such as Global Health Watch, the family-centered nature of the Foundation and the way it is organized makes it unaccountable to those states and people its policies affect.[66] Global Health Watch has found the foundation to be "domineering," "controlling," and monopolizing of agendas through the Health 8 and its wider investment in certain types of research that skews funding for alternative health issues.[67] Feedback and transparency structures are unclear, with responsibility for failed or problematic projects being very much with the grant recipient, partner organization, or state. Part of the issue of accountability is the "venture philanthropy" nature of the foundation's agenda for global health and its links to the private sector. The Bill and Melinda Gates Foundation is different from other foundations that have a tendency to support the arts and further education, yet is similar in that foundation money has often been acquired through tax exemption and in some instances, avoidance. A key problem for the Gates Foundation has been the contradiction between its charitable work and that of Microsoft. According to Global Health Watch, Microsoft was a significant actor in pushing through the TRIPs agreement that has restricted access to medicine in developing countries, and is lobbying to strengthen intellectual property rights further.[68] In January 2007, the *LA Times* published an article that suggested the Foundation funded companies whose activities were contrary to the Foundation's charitable goals;[69] "these businesses include major polluters in the developing world and pharmaceutical companies who have sought to restrict access to much-needed drugs."[70] In a study conducted by Global Health Watch, it was found that despite the Foundation stating they would review their policy in light of such claims, no such change has occurred.[71]

A further problem levied against the Foundation is the shift towards results-based frameworks and the replication of successful models. The benefits of these approaches are clear to see: global health money should go to successful projects where progress and results can be clearly seen and monitored; moreover, these projects can also provide models for other interventions. As one representative from the Gates Foundation puts it "I think that it's a bit odd really that the burden of proof is on this side of the argument."[72] However, results-based strategies run the risk of sidelining those health issues that do not demonstrate an adequate return on donor's investment or providing interventions into health initiatives such as community home-based care, whose value is enormous in impact and delivery of health services as well as impossible to measure. Hence, any widespread shift to these strategies—which as Chapter 5 suggests is a common movement—would be detrimental to a balance towards those health issues that present grey areas in terms of funding outcomes. The replication of successful models highlights a familiar problem within global health governance: that when something is seen to produce results in one area of global health it is often applied to another area or region with limited impact. Adaptability and flexibility thus become a core concern within the hierarchical, results-based model adapted by the Foundation.

Despite being a relatively new actor within global health governance, the Bill and Melinda Gates Foundation follows several principles familiar to philanthropic foundations of old: it is born out of considerable wealth and a will to address some of the largest concerns in the world, comes from the United States with more flexible tax arrangements for large foundations and philanthropy, and is family run and funded. It is also similar to foundations such as the Rockefeller Foundation for the significant influence it has on global health governance. Private philanthropy has a vital role to play in the financing, direction, and innovation in global health governance because its accountability and representative structures are flexible and not dependent on public funds, and hence domestic politics and public opinion. Where the state or intergovernmental organizations are found wanting, private actors emerge to provide increased funding support, and take risks when interventions have become stagnant or lacking in direction or necessary change. However, such organizations are dependent on the role of the public sector in providing the systems and infrastructure to support such innovations and absorb extra funding within health interventions. The balance comes when decision-making is skewed to favor the projects of specific foundations and partnerships co-opt public sector initiatives within market-based approaches preferred by organizations such as the Gates Foundation. Whilst identifying gaps in the market, and promoting competition in terms of efficiency gains and project selection helps the foundation pitch itself as dynamic with measurable results, it also leads to wider competition among actors as institutions pitch for financial support and excludes the non-measurable. This is a pertinent point when considering the role of public–private partnerships for health that have come to define global health governance in the early 2000s. It is the role of partnerships and new institutional arrangements within global health governance that form the main content of the next chapter on new institutions.

Conclusion

Institutions of global health governance represent a myriad of public and private actors with the common interest of health for all but differing approaches as to how this goal can be reached. The WHO remains the central source of information, legitimacy, and authority on global health governance, yet its claims to knowledge and leadership in setting the direction and agenda of global health has increasingly come under question. The WHO has struggled to adapt to internal institutional inertia and external threats and new health concerns. Economic institutions such as the World Bank and private philanthropic organizations such as the Rockefeller Foundation and the Bill and Melinda Gates Foundation have increasingly challenged the mandate of the WHO and the public health approach to understanding global health and its governance. The "public" aspect of governing global public health remains central to the work of the WHO, UN agencies, and NGOs to some degree, but is second to privatized, results-oriented, market-based approaches to delivery within financial institutions and philanthropic bodies. It is this balance between the public and private, coordination between actors and approaches that has made governing global health a complex interplay between these actors. Compounding such complexity has been the emergence of multiple new actors in the form of partnerships, celebrities, and grandmothers which old intergovernmental institutions have had to (or failed to) adapt to and integrate into their operations. The next chapter outlines the role, purpose, and mandate of these actors and what they suggest about how global health is governed.

3 New actors in global health governance

- **G8/G20**
- **Global Fund to Fight AIDS, Tuberculosis and Malaria**
- **Partnerships**
- **Civil society shift: community groups and grandmothers**
- **Celebrities**
- **Conclusion**

The shift from international to global health governance has opened up space for ideas and the delivery of services to be made by a number of different private, public, state, non-state, and hybrid actors. For some, the last 20 years has been heralded as "the era of partnerships" within global health governance.[1] This chapter builds upon the institutions discussed in Chapter 2, to provide a broader conception of what global health governance is and who the actors that compose it are, where they are located, and what it means for the broader strategies for global health.

The chapter pursues this aim in the following way. First, it considers the role of policy forums such as the G8 and G20, their evolving mandate on health, and how they have contributed to the wider discourse between health and development. In so doing, it considers the origins and functions of the Global Fund to Fight AIDS, Tuberculosis and Malaria (hereafter the Global Fund). Second, the chapter considers new forms of partnership supported by the Bill and Melinda Gates Foundation and states to produce new technologies and vaccines to address large health concerns. These partnerships are the International AIDS Vaccine Initiative (IAVI), the Global Alliance for Vaccines and Immunisation (GAVI), and UNITAID. Third, the chapter explores the shift in attention towards civil society organizations away from international non-governmental organizations (NGOs), towards more community-based initiatives. Finally, the chapter considers a contentious and emerging arena of health governance: celebrities. This section explores the role of high-profile celebrities in popular media in contrast to the role and influence of institutional celebrities and charismatic leaders.

G8/G20

The G8 is an informal meeting of the heads of state of eight governments and their financial advisors with the principal purpose of discussing matters of finance and the state of the global economy. Notoriously exclusive and closed from public scrutiny, the G8 countries—the United States, Russia, Japan, Canada, the United Kingdom, France, Italy, and Germany—come together to agree on common goals and policies away from formal mechanisms of decision-making. This allows for frank discussion and face-to-face contact between world leaders. Discussions surrounding the powers of the G8 have been mixed, with some suggesting it is little more than a talking shop and others seeing it as having the ability to set global agendas. Health is a clear example of this latter understanding. Since 1980 the G8 has made 234 specific commitments to health,[2] the most significant of which has been the commitment to establish a global fund for health. For some, the G8's recognition of global health as an important issue has raised health from a state-based development concern to a prominent issue of global foreign policy and international affairs.[3] This section explores the evolution of the G8's role in global health, the increasing presence of the G20 within this, and its wider implications for global health governance.

Global health was initially mooted on the agenda of the then G7 in the 1979 Tokyo Summit, where leaders committed to working with developing countries to overcome malnutrition.[4] From this point onwards, health was seen as one issue among many to be supported by the G7 through the United Nations (UN) system based on state support to the World Health Organization (WHO) in terms of financing and the surveillance of emerging and existing health threats and concerns. It was not until the mid 1990s that the G8 started to focus on health through its relationship to international development and the welfare of developing countries.[5] The 1996 Lyon Summit marked a shift in this regard, away from the WHO-centered approach to health interventions initially favored by the G8 towards a more substantive appraisal of the socio-economic drivers and consequences of ill-health. As Kirton and Kakotsis describe, it was at this point that the G8 found its voice on global health.[6] During this period the G8 began to recognize its potential role and responsibilities within global health. However beyond the inclusion of health concerns within its discussions, the G8 only engaged in health interventions and delivery primarily through specialized agencies within the UN system.

It was not until the early 2000s that the G8 began to develop its own system of health interventions beyond the UN. The primary example of this has been the Global Fund. The Global Fund was created out of a US$1.3 billion commitment to combat the three diseases by G8 members at the Genoa Summit in 2001. This commitment happened alongside several other high policy statements on health, vaccine initiatives, and wider engagement with the pharmaceutical sector towards affordable medicine.[7] Infectious disease remained at the core of the G8's agenda during the early to mid 2000s, as highlighted in the 2003 Evian Summit communiqué, 2004 Sea Island Summit emphasis on HIV and polio vaccines, 2005 Gleneagles focus on Africa, and 2006 St Petersburg summit's use of infectious disease as one of its main priority areas.[8] The emphasis on health, specifically the three diseases, was part of a wider focus towards the "social" aspects of development, particularly in sub-Saharan Africa in line with the UN Millennium Development Goals (MDGs). This period marked a turning point both for the governance of global health and for the G8 in regards to the shift from providing financial support for UN agencies to the creation of new institutional arrangements to channel and spend money.

Commitments to diseases, particularly HIV/AIDS, have been motivated by individual leaders soliciting political will at the G8 meetings. As with many global issues, getting an item on the political agenda depends on the political will of individuals within positions of power and civil society backing to push for them. The flexibility of the G8 opens it up to direct influence of particular state and non-state actors in putting an issue on the table. Within the G8 this occurs through state leaders, their "sherpas" who target particular parts of the wider G8 membership bureaucracy ahead of the summit, and international institutions such as the World Bank that help elicit widespread support, particularly among developing countries.[9] According to Kirton *et al.*, when particular states are less forthcoming about certain issues, leaders can go outside of the G8 to use monitoring agencies to track and gain wider compliance.[10] Hence, the rise of global health within the G8 is based on the ability to frame issues alongside the wider objectives of the summit, and base developments on a cumulative approach to an issue. Issues of global health have been effectively snowballed within the G8's wider agenda, from basic importance within the summit communiqués, to commitments to pre-existing UN agencies, to the formation and sustained support for institutions independent of the UN.

The impact of the G8 in putting specific issues onto the global agenda and establishing new, well-funded global health institutions such as the Global Fund raises questions over the "good" governance and transparency of this summit and its wider implications for global health governance. Fundamentally for a body with considerable leverage over the global health agenda, the G8 is characterized by a significant accountability and transparency deficit, and maintains the state as the central focus of global health governance in terms of direction and policy decision-making.[11] The first problem with the G8 is the nature of their commitments to health, and the source and type of money allocated to health financing. For many, the "new" funds earmarked to combat global health issues are recycled forms of debt relief.[12] New financial commitments made to global health are channeled through old institutions and structures such as the World Bank, that as Chapter 2 has highlighted, have often been seen to have policies that have negatively impacted upon health outcomes.[13] The use of such institutions often leads to health initiatives being tied to conditionalities[14] and wider processes of structural reform within a state. Second, beyond who allocates and structures the G8's initiatives, there is an issue on how the money is spent. The G8 has focused a great deal on vertical interventions into big diseases, and has been instrumental in placing issues such as HIV/AIDS at the top of the political agenda which to some extent acts to the detriment of neglected diseases or health system strengthening. The focus of G8 interventions has been less the health concerns of their own populations such as alcoholism and obesity but more towards those of developing countries, who are under-represented within this forum. According to Labonte and Schrecker, an additional criticism of the G8's role in global health has been the general unwillingness to tackle fundamental and often contentious problems such as the brain drain and the socio-economic determinants of health.[15] This leads to a fourth criticism of the G8, it engages in health as a means of presenting itself as a non-political "force for good" in the world. Health has come onto the agenda of the G8 at a time of sustained criticism of the institution, it is key to the repositioning of the G8 as not a secretive, capitalist entity, but a forum for discussion as to how to solve the world's common problems. Health is not fundamental to the G8's agenda, and whilst it remains a relevant area of policy, it will always be on a second tier to issues of the global political economy.

Criticisms aside, the actions of the G8 have had fundamental reverberations in the priorities, institutions, and funding commitments of global health governance. For global health to be sustained as part of the G8's agenda, it has to be recognized by the G20 states—G8 + Argentina, Australia, Brazil, China, India, Indonesia, Mexico, Russia, Saudi Arabia, South Africa, the Republic of Korea, and Turkey. Similar to the G8, the G20 was formed to discuss issues pertaining to the global financial system, principally arising from the financial crises of the 1990s and their impact on parts of Latin America and developing countries. These states, particularly Brazil, China, India, and Saudi Arabia, are being looked to by health-specific agencies such as the Global Fund and WHO as key sources of future health financing. The G8/G20 perform an effective signaling leadership function that overcomes the institutional statis and restrictions on funding that have blocked some of the old institutions of global health, making it "a useful supplement, gap filler, and insurance policy for an inadequate WHO."[16] The most obvious of this that encapsulates these issues and the G8's approach to tackling global health issues has been the Global Fund.

The Global Fund to Fight AIDS, Tuberculosis and Malaria

The Global Fund is the clearest representation of changes in global health financing and decision-making since the late 1990s. Established in 2002, the Global Fund is a funding mechanism to support country-based interventions into the "big three" diseases—HIV/AIDS, malaria, and tuberculosis. Similar to most institutions of global health, the Fund is run by a working secretariat based in Geneva and a board of directors. Different to other actors in global health, the Fund's board of directors is made up of a combination of donor states, multilateral partners, *and* representatives of civil society and the private sector. It is this model of partnership and inclusion of non-state actors in decision-making that marks new institutions of global health out from the old. The secretariat, headed by the office of the executive director manages the day-to-day running of the fund and funding distribution activities. The Global Fund has no institutional in-country presence. Instead it works through country coordinating mechanisms (CCMs) made up of governments, the private sector, and civil society who review funding applications and manage funding dispersal to the principal and sub-recipients of Fund money. The Global Fund identifies the CCMs' core role as being: i) to "co-ordinate the development and submission of national proposals;" ii) "nominate the principal recipient" of Fund money who will then work closely with the sub-recipients in the implementation of the grant; iii) "oversee implementation"; iv) "approve any reprogramming"; and v) "ensure linkages and consistency between Global Fund grants and other national health and development programmes."[17] In effect this means that the CCMs operate as over-seers of the Fund process to make sure that grants reflect the interests of the state they contribute to and do so in a way that develops previous Global Fund work within that country.

The lack of a clear institutional presence means the fund is reliant on effective partnerships with both the membership of the CCMs, local fund agents, and donor partners such as UN agencies, the World Bank, and bilateral donors in-country. In practice, these bodies act as the eyes and ears of the Fund on the ground: the operational aspect of the Global Fund relies on partnerships for effective project implementation, funding support and advocacy. The Joint United Nations Programme on HIV/AIDS (UNAIDS), the World Bank, WHO, and Roll Back Malaria all have non-voting representation on the board. They are integral to the fund's future direction and mandate, and work in an advisory capacity to senior management. As well as including other agencies within its central mechanisms, participants from the Global Fund have a mission briefing team to the World Health Assembly (WHA), and at the UN General Assembly at key times, for example, at the 2010 MDG summit, and at the World Bank.[18] The fund's relationship with its partners is in many ways codependent: it needs these agencies in terms of technical capacity and in-country presence and knowledge, and in turn the agencies need the fund in terms of financial resources. The one area of partnership that remains under-developed is that between the fund and bilateral partners. Although bilateral donors are represented on the board and are key to the fund's replenishment this is an area to be developed by the fund, specifically in the area of information sharing and technical expertise, to the same degree that characterizes the fund's relationship with multilateral agencies.[19]

No formal in-country presence is key to the role of the fund in global health. The Global Fund positions itself as a source of finance for interventions into HIV/AIDS, tuberculosis, and malaria; it has no other claims to knowledge, expertise, coordination, or recommendations. It is very much an actor that generates funding to support and facilitate country ownership of programs. The fund receives money from bilateral donors, foundations, corporations such as Chevron, large NGOs such as Comic Relief, pharmaceutical companies, and product funding such as the MAC AIDS Fund and Product (RED). The fund works in partnership with institutions such as the World Bank, UNITAID, and GAVI in mobilizing resources, coordination, civil society relations, and lobbying of governments. Similar to most new health actors, the fund has promoted "innovative" forms of funding. One such mechanism is the Dow Jones Global Fund 50 Index, which measures the performance of the largest companies that support the mission of the Global Fund. A portion of revenues generated through the licensing of the index will go to the fund.[20]

Civil society organizations are central to the operations of the Global Fund. Beyond their presence on the board, civil society actors have to be included in country grant proposals and strategies and represented within the CCMs. Civil society actors in the form of NGOs tend to fulfill the role of sub-recipients of Global Fund grants, but are increasingly pushing to become principal recipients.[21] Beyond the implementation and decision-making aspects of this relationship, the Global Fund engages with civil society organizations through in-country strengthening of inclusion in formal processes, advocacy, and building relations between the state and the community by civil society specialists based in Geneva.[22] These actors try to identify the needs of civil society actors in country, and strengthen their collaboration both within Global Fund processes such as the CCMs, as well as beyond these formal arrangements. The presence and influence of civil society organizations within the fund's activities often depends on the region in which it operates. For example in the Latin America and Caribbean region, civil society actors make up the majority of principle recipients[23]whereas in parts of Western Africa they mainly occupy the role of sub-recipients and are less likely to engage in advocacy.[24] This in the main reflects the nature of state-civil society relations within specific countries and the history of non-state involvement; it also reflects the governance practices associated with the three diseases. For example, some of the Global Fund's activities have been more swayed towards HIV/AIDS as civil society has been more organized in lobbying states and advocating for better treatment and care for people living with HIV. Hence on most CCMs, NGOs tend to be more representative of HIV than malaria or TB,[25] yet there is a growing spillover effect of such representation into the other two diseases.

The Global Fund has had two executive directors: Richard Feachem (2002–7) and Michel Kazatchkine (2007–). Feachem's background is in medicine, global health and development, with experience working in institutes for global health at the London School of Hygiene and Tropical Medicine and the University of California, San Francisco, as well as health policy experience in the Health, Nutrition and Population sector of the World Bank. Feachem was instrumental in shaping the fund's initial portfolio that emphasized "middle-sized" project-based funding with less coherence or over-arching strategy to the programmes it funded other than to support community and state-based initiatives where it was most needed. Similar to Feachem, Kazatchkine comes from a medical background, with experience in health diplomacy, specifically within the WHO. The appointment of Kazatchkine in 2007 saw the fund's funding portfolio grow from US$10.1 billion in 2007 to US$19.3 billion in 2010,[26] staff numbers increase, as well as a change in approach towards a business model that emphasizes efficiency savings and results-oriented frameworks for funding support as a means of maximizing the Fund's impact.

Conscious of changes in health and development funding, and its position and longevity, the Fund is now much keener to promote its involvement in health system strengthening and more joined up interventions in health more broadly. In this sense the Fund has shifted from a more adaptable, flexible funding institution, to one which is more focused on procedure and controls on managing the fund's activities.[27] The result of this performance-based approach for many working at and with the fund has been positive, and adapted by other partnerships and institutions working on global health issues to represent a "change of paradigm."[28] The shift away from project–project funding towards more streamlined, related, efficiency approaches to conducting the fund's work was as one senior staff member of the fund describes, Kazatchkine's "vision, where he wants to go, tracking how we work … and this is a huge repackaging on what the staff is."[29] Central to this repackaging has been the fund's institutional independence. From January 2009, the Fund became administratively autonomous from the WHO allowing its working structures in terms of staffing, procurement, and finance to adapt separately to the WHO's.

The Global Fund has made the following impact on global health governance. First, it has mobilized a considerable amount of resources for HIV/AIDS, tuberculosis, and malaria from both private and public sources in a relatively short period of time. This shows that there is political will and support to address global health concerns. However, this will centers upon specific concerns, and as such the fund has led to a distortion on what is prioritized in global health, with "the big three" being the subject of most interventions. The fund has shifted towards more holistic approaches that include elements of health system strengthening, but this remains a contentious issue within the board and hence the mandate of the institution remains the three diseases. Second, other than the International Labour Organization (ILO), the Global Fund represents one of the only global institutions that involve equal voting rights between state and non-state representatives. In this sense it is the most progressive global health institution in regards to multisectoralism and civil society participation. This approach has become a defining feature of governing global health, with older institutions such as the WHO having to adapt to and adopt wider inclusionary practice towards civil society. Third, the fund has established results and performance-based initiatives as a working central operating principle of global health financing. This is central to the ability to sustain financing for global health to show that funding can work and produce results if sustained. However, such results-based approaches have to be complemented by more flexible funding structures, as some initiatives integral to combating the three diseases, such as long-term attitude change to stigma and denial in regards to HIV become increasingly hard to measure or quantify. Finally, the Global Fund has represented a shift in institutional arrangements towards country ownership by presenting itself as a funding-only Geneva-based body with no in-country presence.

Health system strengthening, institutional rivalry, and the lack of in-country presence remain the central contentions within the fund. The Global Fund has a larger budget than many "old" global health institutions, but still has to rely on such institutions for support in its operations. This can lead to strain and jealousy among partners. It is frustrating for both those in-country and for staff members within the fund to not have continued presence in-country as there is a general feeling that some areas or people are not reached; information goes unshared or becomes too filtered; certain issues become distorted or lost in communication; and more straightforward problems with implementation become difficult to address.[30] CCMs have had problems with efficiency, capacity, and a lack of a solution-oriented approach to problem-solving.[31] The lack of in-country presence can restrict the fund's direct control of in-house monitoring and evaluation systems. While the fund has rigorous monitoring and evaluation systems, these are reliant on information from in-country partners, and hence position the fund as an easy target for criticism when challenges of corruption arise. Despite some seeing this as a "weak point"[32] of the fund opinion within the fund tends to balance it against the idea that it is the only way of fully promoting country ownership. In the short term, it represents a shift in burden from the fund to its in-country partners and the government in which it works.

The future of the Global Fund in part relies on its ability to overcome these key contentions and secure sustained funding for the management and expansion of its programs. For the Global Fund to become the significant actor that its board and management seek to position it as, depends on the re-positioning of the fund beyond the dominance of HIV and AIDS, and addressing its "global" nature and the eligibility of certain regions where the epidemics are not as big. Constraints or larger contributions to the Fund's replenishment rounds will in part make the solutions to these contentions more obvious. For many the fund will have to broaden its mandate to stay relevant in the context of the other health-related MDGs[33] but it will do so at a time when we see a turning point when the Global Fund has received US$10 billion less than it had planned for in its 2010 replenishment pledges.

Partnerships

As the previous section demonstrated, the core organization of the Global Fund has been around partnership. For many, the shift from international to global health has been marked by the rise and difference in "innovative" partnerships, from public–private partnerships (PPPs) to product-development partnerships, and vaccine initiatives. PPPs are prominent features of global governance more broadly; however, the number, scope, and scale of these partnerships are particularly acute within global health governance. Partnerships have become integral to the strategies of institutions such as the WHO and an example to other areas of global politics that collective action beyond the state is effective and efficient. This section considers the definition, role, and origin of these partnerships in global health, before focusing on three of the largest PPPs—the GAVI, IAVI, and UNITAID. Disease-specific partnerships such as Roll Back Malaria and Stop TB are discussed in more detail in Chapter 5.

The central operating part of PPPs is that they are a combination of state and non-state actors derived from international institutions, states, civil society, and the private sector that organize in a flexible manner around specific issues or objectives of global health. Depending on the size of the partnership, they tend to have an institutional base in the offices of one of the established global health partners if small and a standalone office in a key headquarters of global health such as Geneva. The stated benefits of PPPs are that they tend to be results-oriented, and have clearly defined and regulated outputs built on a business model of project development[34] that sees a clear relationship between supply and demand.[35] Objectives tend to be defined by the public side of the partnerships by the institutions and states involved, with risk and responsibility falling more to the private aspect in terms of service delivery and support for clearly identified outcomes.[36] In regards to health, PPPs have concentrated on product development, new vaccines and medicines, information systems, and incentives for industry.[37] As such the focus of such partnerships has been towards vertical interventions for disease eradication, from the big three, to increasingly neglected disease. One of their central roles, however, has been to generate, sustain, and offer alternatives in all-important funding for health issues. These funding mechanisms can often sit in stark contrast to under-funded UN bodies and thus offer them an alternative source of resource mobilization.[38]

The inclusion of PPPs for health has been driven by multiple bilateral and multilateral agencies such as the UK Department for International Development (DFID), and the United States Agency for International Development (USAID), the World Bank, and the Rockefeller Foundation. PPPs became a prominent part of the global health agenda towards the end of the 1990s: Gro Harlem Brundtland's first speech at the WHO in 1998 emphasized the need for wider partnerships and relationships with the private sector[39] and the World Bank began to link PPPs to its wider approach to comprehensive development and market-oriented approaches to global health governance. This period saw the emergence of multiple partnerships for health from the WHO's 1999 guidelines for collaboration with the private sector, to more institutionalized partnerships such as the 1995 PolioPlus Campaign.[40] The degree to which institutions engage with PPPs for health depends on the type of organization, its mandate, and culture of working with the private sector in a mutual partnership. A key PPP formed during the mid-late 1990s was IAVI.

IAVI

Established in 1996 as a result of the Rockefeller Foundation's drive for an HIV vaccine, the purpose of the IAVI was to generate political support for a vaccine, create a vaccine, and then identify the arrangements whereby the vaccine would be distributed, a key part of which being who would receive the vaccine first and where. According to Chataway *et al.*, the IAVI works with governments, NGOs, pharmaceutical companies, multilateral and bilateral donors to find a common voice when advocating for the need for a vaccine and new mechanisms or funding strategies to meet this need.[41] A core function of the IAVI's mandate, which those working for the institution are keen to stress, is working with local communities and governments throughout the world to sensitize people to vaccine trials and identify how a vaccine will be distributed, on what grounds, the cost, and who pays that cost. In this sense, the IAVI's main role is to act as a mechanism that fosters support, knowledge, and expertise, and finds a medium in which different approaches and mandates can come together.

Organizationally, the IAVI has an institutional basis in New York, with an executive office in Manhattan and laboratories in Brooklyn, and regional offices in Kenya, Uganda, India, South Africa, Amsterdam, and the United Kingdom. Beyond these institutional areas, the work of the IAVI in terms of vaccine research and clinical trials operates in 23 states.[42] The initiative was initially funded by a combination of the Rockefeller and Bill and Melinda Gates Foundations, the World Bank, the DFID, USAID, and the Swedish International Development Cooperation Agency (SIDA).[43] However, its current funding pool has been extended to include various different bilateral aid agencies, the EU, corporate sector partners such as GoogleInc and Pfizer, individuals, foundations such as the Until There's a Cure Foundation, and matching campaigns.[44]

The IAVI is a significant actor in global health because of its ability to bring together actors who would ordinarily be seen to have opposing views. In this sense it laid the foundation for larger, more institutionalized partnerships in bringing participants from government, civil society, and the private sector together. The ability of the IAVI to do so has come from the credibility it had from its founding donor the Rockefeller Foundation, the momentum of support it was able to generate, and how it has positioned itself as an expertised partnership that is the go-to initiative for vaccine research and knowledge. This partnership and expertise has given IAVI state and non-state legitimacy in promoting its agenda, advocating for a vaccine, and demonstrating its worth in global health governance. However, its autonomy and influence on vaccine research and the institutional arrangements around access are limited to sustained funding and an equal balance within the partnership. The IAVI is of significant size for a partnership; however, its budget and remit is dwarfed by other national health agencies.[45] The IAVI has to assert its relevance within a system of competing budgets and national interests that may defend specific health budgets and initiatives and attempt to safeguard funding for their own scientific research centers. Its research and knowledge base in this regard is only as good as the donor support and state-based laboratories and trials it advocates for and supports. Although the IAVI prioritizes the issue of who receives the vaccine, how, at what cost, and who meets that cost, there are no clear answers to these questions and should a vaccine be identified, we would be no further in identifying such allocation processes than before the IAVI was established.

GAVI Alliance

The Global Alliance for Vaccines and Immunization or "the GAVI alliance" has a similar purpose to the IAVI in terms of advocating for new vaccines research and supply, as well as highlighting the need for sustained financing, and access strategies in this regard. It takes the need for equity, country ownership, and performance-based results delivered in a "financially sustainable" "innovative business model" way[46] that is similar to many partnership arrangements. However, GAVI's remit is broader than finding a vaccine just for HIV or malaria and tuberculosis, with a specific focus on new and underused vaccines for a broad arena of health concerns. In addition, GAVI shows a wider commitment towards health system strengthening as an integral part of immunization strategies.

Established in 2000, the purpose of GAVI was to initially strengthen vaccine delivery systems, develop new vaccines, and highlight and promote underused vaccines as a means of scaling up immunization programs in developing countries. This remains the main focus of GAVI's agenda; however, it has also looked to ways in which it can sustain funding levels, speed up price reductions, and work with countries to manage the competing demands often put upon them by donors. This has led to two developments in sustaining funds: the International Finance Facility for Immunization (IFFIm) and the Advance Market Commitment (AMC). The purpose of the IFFIm is to elicit 10–20-year donor commitments which are then leveraged in capital markets to support the immunization of 500 million children against measles, tetanus, and yellow fever. By 2010, GAVI has been able to raise US$1 billion.[47] The AMC concentrates on the affordability of vaccines and the provision of access for all, particularly those in low- and middle-income countries, whilst maintaining suitable return for those countries that develop them. The AMC rests on a pre-arrangement by donors to set the price of vaccines before they have been developed. It has been argued that this mechanism provides pharmaceutical companies with "a huge carrot by subsidizing the initial purchase of new vaccines for the poor, if they vow to sell those vaccines cheaply in the future."[48]

In addition to new funding mechanisms, GAVI receives funding from donor countries and its partners, specifically the Bill and Melinda Gates Foundation, the World Bank, UNICEF, and WHO. These partners have a place on the board of GAVI alongside two civil society representatives, two industry members, one person from a research institute, five industrialized states, and four developing country representatives. Beyond the partners, the members of the board have a rotating membership. As with most partnerships, beyond the board, the day-to-day activities are run by the GAVI secretariat.

What makes GAVI stand out among comparable partnerships has been its ability to leverage additional funds through sovereign pledges to elicit wider money from capital markets. Whilst other partnerships have adopted business models in terms of management, innovation in corporate social responsibility, and implementation, GAVI has been the first partnership to fully undergo a process of financialization in support of its activities. This allows GAVI to sustain funds beyond donor support, but as with processes of financialization such leverage can come at a risk. For some, GAVI is at odds with the WHO's broader commitment to universal access and equity in medicine and vaccine distribution.[49] The introduction of the market to incentivize investment in vaccine research and leverage money to support such research can ultimately lead to a distortion in how vaccines are distributed, priced, and who pays for them. For some this should be limited by the presence of civil society actors, and common partners across PPPs such as UNITAID, IAVI, and the Global Fund. However, similar to IAVI, there remains no common agreement as to price, and where the price is agreed it can be held to ransom should the cost of producing the vaccine not be as high as initially expected. Hence, vaccines may not be distributed as early as possible as companies try to demonstrate a greater investment in research and development that may be the case. To maintain its commitment to equity this is a key factor that GAVI must address.

UNITAID

UNITAID is a partnership with the stated aim of increasing access to treatment for HIV, malaria, and tuberculosis through "innovative" financing such as air travel tax, and more contentious models such as patent pools. It presents itself as an international drug purchase facility that similar to other partnerships works with governments, NGOs, international organizations, and pharmaceutical companies to increase drug availability in developing countries. The idea for UNITAID was founded by the French and Brazilian governments who lobbied within the UN system for wider access to medicine, specifically in poorer countries where the need was greatest. With the support of an additional 44 countries, UNITAID was launched in the UN General Assembly in September 2006. Based at the WHO offices in Geneva, UNITAID takes a standard partnership form of being governed by an executive board made up of state and civil society representatives, chair and WHO representative; a secretariat chaired by an Executive Secretary and consisting of the secretary's office and operations; and three working groups. Actors familiar to new partnerships such as the World Bank, UNICEF, and UNAIDS as well as the Global Fund, Stop TB, Roll Back Malaria, the Clinton HIV/AIDS Initiative, and the Foundation for Innovative New Diagnostics (FIND) are the main partners of the organization.

UNITAID is funded by taxes on air travel—either through tickets for air travel, or from broader taxes on carbon dioxide emissions—as well as donor budget contributions, which combined have led to total contributions of US$1.5 billion since its inception.[50] Twenty-nine countries have agreed to tax flights leaving their countries according to destination, ticket class, and budgetary contributions.[51] This funding commitment is set to increase under the remit of UNITAID's "massivegood" project, with the introduction of donation opportunities when booking flights through ticket-issuers and travel portals.[52] UNITAID has two main functions. The first is to use the money it raises to provide affordable treatment to low- and middle-income countries through accelerated and expanded delivery and supply. Second, UNITAID directly engages with those issues of intellectual property and patent protection discussed in Chapter 2 through its patent pool initiative. The purpose of this initiative is to encourage pharmaceutical companies to make their patents available before their 20-year expiry. In so doing, the pool aims to facilitate the development of cheaper drugs for treatment of "the big three."

UNITAID's record in fulfilling its objectives has been mixed. Since the creation of the patent pool in 2008 some pharmaceutical companies have pledged to renew their stance on patent protection in regards to HIV, malaria, and tuberculosis drugs. However, despite support from the western media and complementary NGO campaigns, there continues to be a lack of match between words and deeds on the part of patent availability. Drug prices have fallen but this is a result of subsidies from organizations such as UNITAID and the Clinton HIV/AIDS Initiative and the end of old drug patents. Poor access to high-quality products through a fully functioning patent pool is yet to be realized. These issues are ongoing and UNITAID has made some progress in its early stages. However, political will, funding commitments, demand, and supply mechanisms need to be maintained for affordable drugs to become more available in the future.

H8

The most recent, informal, and secretive partnership is the Health 8 or the "H8." Made up of the Bill and Melinda Gates Foundation, the World Bank, the WHO, UNICEF, UNFPA, UNAIDS, GAVI, and the Global Fund, the H8 has a similar rationale for health as the G8/G20 has for global finance: it is established to provide an informal cooperation forum where institutions can share ideas, knowledge, and provide a common strategy for combating some of the world's largest health concerns. A significant difference from the G8, however, is that it is composed of institutions, not states. For many this reflects a defining feature of global health governance—that it is organized around institutions as opposed to state interests. The H8 supports this notion and furthers institutional autonomy from member states as they collectively lobby for specific health issues to be raised and funding sustained. For some the H8 represents an effective alignment and coordination between organizations and thus is a good example for the formation of global regimes organized around specific issue areas that do not rely on states to drive the agenda. On the other hand, with perhaps the exception of the Bill and Melinda Gates Foundation, these institutions still remain bound by the decisions and contributions of member states, and thus only engage in a limited form of autonomy from those that fund them and sit on their boards. Whilst the H8 presents the notion of cooperation, in practice this does not necessarily happen operationally, with divides between old and new actors in global health. Part of this division is because of the large budgetary support new actors receive, but also because these new actors lack legitimacy and representation. Where old institutions such as the WHO are answerable to their member states and their electorates—albeit indirectly—new actors such as the GAVI only remain accountable to those bodies that fund it and the institutions that make up the partnership. The H8 may present a new paradigm in institutional collaboration, but in many ways it reflects the old system of the state-based G8 in terms of lack of transparency, accountability, and representation.

Civil society shift: community groups and grandmothers

The role of the community—individuals, family members, and neighbors—has become a central element of global health governance. The community has always played an active role in the delivery of services, especially during times of public sector spending cuts for health. However, this has become more acute with the shift from international to global health governance and an emphasis on decentralization and community-led responses.

The common purpose to the rise of partnerships and new actors has been to decentralize global health governance and make it less hierarchical. Communities are seen to have the best knowledge as to the health concerns of their local populations, and in engaging in delivery of support systems are better placed to identify their needs. Rightly or wrongly global health policy has increasingly positioned communities as the legitimate sites of health delivery and knowledge. The perceived lack of accountability within international non-governmental organizations (INGOs) and legitimizing of community activity have led to a drive by intergovernmental organizations towards cutting out the middle INGOs to fund and partner local communities directly. INGOs and states still have a role in facilitating such relationships; however, the focus is very much on community-led, community-based, inclusive initiatives. Hence, to demonstrate legitimacy and accountability, INGOs, states, and international institutions must closely align their operations to local communities, as well as facilitating the participation of such communities in wider policy-making circles.

This focus on the community has been met by large-scale funding initiatives from the Global Fund, PPPs, and the World Bank to precipitate and sustain community participation in global health governance. Funding has been channeled in the first instance to service delivery and specific projects, but has also centered on new participatory forums for community groups in state-based and global decision-making fora. The purpose of this is to sustain those at the frontline of health service delivery, or acting within wider support structures such as grandmothers looking after large numbers of orphans. Grandmothers have become emblematic of the new agency assigned to the role of communities and individuals. Community groups and individuals have always had agency as active citizens with an impact and role on their immediate, localized surroundings; yet this agency has often been used by other actors as a means of legitimizing their actions or policies, rather than communities or grandmothers themselves using such agency to project their knowledge and experience to global policy-making circles. Funding bodies such as the Stephen Lewis Foundation have given a great deal of attention to these women, highlighting their commitment and role, and stressing the need to support them, and crucially not to view their labor and commitment as free.

The issue of free labor remains a central contention within global health governance. The form of agency ascribed to communities and individuals is that of the unpaid volunteer. Funding to these actors finance the activity, not the labor cost or support structures that deliver services. Hence, although inclusion and focus on the community suggests a "new" role for local actors in global health governance, it continues to rest on the individual and the family as the giver of free support and services. In practice, the providers of such services are women, girls, and grandmothers. Community-based health governance can maintain a system that rests on the free provision of labor at the local level, with individual and community responsibility being used as a buffer for public spending in global health. "The community" and "grandmothers" occupy a convenient position for channeling money towards decentralized global health initiatives. However, communities are often the last to see or receive such funds, and often complain of delays and bureaucracy in accessing decision-making forums or funding rounds. Community groups continue to have their "global" status ascribed to them by the international institutions that fund them, yet fair or sustained participation in decision-making is limited. Communities, families, and individuals have an important role and value in global health governance, yet such a role is often put upon such actors, especially in developing countries, with old institutions of global health governance often failing to fully support them.

Celebrities

Central to the governance of global health has been the rise of celebrity involvement in issue-raising, agenda-setting, and "celebrity diplomacy."[53] Global health governance has had its own specific brand of "health celebrity" within institutions when considering the role of Peter Piot in UNAIDS, Richard Feachem within the Global Fund, and multiple directors-general of the WHO in shaping the agenda of these institutions and global health more broadly. However, increasingly the notion of global health celebrity has been extended to more public personalities that recognize health as an interesting arena in which to promote their philanthropic endeavors or personal cause. According to Street, celebrities have been involved in domestic politics and local agendas in one of two ways: i) those elected officials who engage within popular culture to enhance specific political goals or ii) entertainers who make pronouncements on politics, make public gestures or statements, or make claims to represent a specific issue/people.[54] Based on these definitions, celebrity politics generally refers to the overlap between politics and popular culture or political representation as a cultural act.[55] In this sense, celebrity diplomacy is not new. However, what is new is the rise in number and type of celebrity organized to target global health. According to looktothestars.org, a database of celebrity giving, health is the second highest cause (with children being the number one) of celebrities. Health in many ways occupies a non-political position for celebrities, as they tend not to address the social, economic, and political drivers of ill-health. Celebrities instead support a particular health campaign or short-term strategy whilst maintaining their apolitical status, and thus not alienating their core fan base by going "too radical" or "too political." Health allows celebrities to engage in global issues, appear altruistic and giving, as well as serious and somewhat intellectual for their understanding of complex issues. Fundamentally, it raises their profile.

The benefits of celebrity involvement for global health governance relate to wider and deeper awareness of and fundraising for specific health issues. Celebrities are able to gain wider coverage of certain issues to a much broader audience and are a useful tool for gaining media publicity. Celebrities give institutions additional leverage to bargain and negotiate with states, from the publicity and information sharing that they generate and public support they can engender. In this sense, celebrities do not have an independent agency within global health governance, but are a useful tool of intergovernmental organizations such as the WHO and UNAIDS, and alliances such as the Global Fund to boost their global exposure. Further to the role they have within institutional bargaining and soft diplomacy, celebrities play a key function in awareness and behavior change communication in regard to specific health issues such as HIV/AIDS. Celebrities in the form of singers, actors, models, and sports people can act as role models for learnt behavior, and are able to communicate forms of behavior change among fans.

Celebrity involvement in global health governance takes the following forms. The first is perhaps the most traditional, institutionalized form, that of Goodwill Ambassadors for UN institutions. The role of these ambassadors is to strengthen and raise awareness of specific health issues. Goodwill Ambassadors are selected from a range of backgrounds[56] with different commitments and uses for the role. The role has loose criteria, and is as effective as specific celebrities want it to be, depending on their time, interest, and other commitments. The concept of a Goodwill Ambassador has extended to the national level, with nationally appointed ambassadors engaging in awareness raising in-country and then feeding back to global initiatives. Pu Cunxin, a popular Chinese actor, has acted as an AIDS activist both within China and ambassador for China's HIV/AIDS response at the local and global level. He has been pivotal in combating stigma surrounding the disease in China, as well as using his experiences to heighten awareness within global institutions. For China, he is a positive export in wider policymaking and diplomacy circles in this regard. Beyond Goodwill Ambassadors and intergovernmental institutions, celebrities engage with global health through collaborations with NGOs. Such collaborations are also predominantly about awareness raising for specific health issues, as well as the work of an NGO as a means of eliciting further donor support. Celebrity fundraising occurs through: direct donations; establishment of a fund or foundation in the celebrity's name, for example, the

Michael J Fox Foundation; high-profile fundraising events, for example, Elton John's White Tie and Tiara Ball; participation in fundraising concerts/telethons, for example, Live Aid and Live 8; or publicity for specific campaigns. Relationships with NGOs tend to be the central entry point for celebrities into global health governance. It is from such collaborations that celebrities learn about issues, develop first-hand field experience, and become prominent within the global health governance arena.

The second form celebrity inclusion takes in global health governance is their presence within PPPs such as Product (RED). The role of celebrities in such partnerships is predominantly product promotion as a form of awareness raising and investment in health strategies. Such a role, again, depends on the level of commitment made by the celebrity. For example, in regards to Product (RED) celebrity involvement can range from product promotion, for example, specialist headphones endorsed by musicians Dr Dre and Lady Gaga, to television exposure, for example, reality show "Project Runway" has a challenge to design a (RED) dress for a red carpet event, to more sustained involvement and direction of the campaign from celebrities such as U2 singer Bono. Bono was a pivotal actor in the establishment of Product (RED). Bono has gone beyond institutional inclusion, to carve out a separate identity, and hence form of celebrity diplomacy through his individual style as a "charming fixer."[57] As Youde describes, (RED) does not fundamentally alter the underlying determinants of the HIV/AIDS crisis, or seek to engage with structural issues of global health; but its interest to scholars of international relations and global governance lies in the "coming together of private forces to address public concerns."[58]

The third form of celebrity involvement is those celebrities not involved in the entertainment or sports industries that have a global presence in regards to health issues or past experience in global policymaking. These types of celebrities can be ex-government officials or politicians such as Bill Clinton, ex-UN or World Bank bureaucrats such as Jeffrey Sachs, or perceived experts or activists in the global health field such as Stephen Lewis. These celebrities have a different role than those based in the entertainment and sports industries as they appeal to a different demographic and gain legitimacy from their existing high profile within global policymaking circles and longevity working on specific issues. They tend to be drawn from a wider epistemic community organized around health and are thus familiar to practitioners and often have informal but direct access to policy and decision-making. These celebrities are able to utilize the media, the language of institutions, and strategic relationships whilst maintaining an apolitical, broker role. Similar to entertainment-based celebrities, they have a key role in fundraising, but are different in that they have access to high-profile meetings and decision-making.

The distinction between the two types of celebrity is an important one to make, especially in regard to the limitations of celebrity within global health governance. It is important not to overstate their role. They are predominantly located in awareness and fundraising activities, and very few have agency within global health governance independent of the institutions, partnerships, and alliances they form. For every Bono there is a bandwagon celebrity, and very few, if any, have direct access to decision-making forums. However, the presence of celebrities such as Bono does lead to several issues of concern. These celebrities can distort or hijack a specific agenda, presenting a specific kind of knowledge and information, and crowding out alternative research or perspectives. Celebrity diplomacy can result in further exclusion of marginalized groups, such as women and ethnic minorities to the reproduction and absorption of dominant white, male, middle, or upper class opinion. Further to this, they can oversimplify complex problems. This is in part their role, to make issues digestible to the wider public, yet this is best balanced with thought-through interventions that perpetuate opinion underpinned by consensus and wider research.

Conclusion

New institutions within global health governance represent a move away from intergovernmental state-based actors as the key mechanisms for creating common commitments to global health problems. These institutions involve a shift from the public sector to include private actors in the form of celebrities, partnerships, community organizations, and individuals. However, the most defining feature has been the emergence of PPPs, the growth of which has been stimulated by state-based actors that provide the funding, legitimacy and mandate for such partnerships. Their activities whilst adaptable and results-oriented, rely on the role of state institutions and intergovernmental organizations to implement them and promote ownership. Partnerships allow for wider flexibility and adaptability to global health concerns, and provide a forum in which the scientific developments and biomedical concerns of global health can be balanced alongside more political ideas of justice, liberty, and fairness. Yet, they lack a degree of legitimacy, transparency, and representation to the people they affect, becoming answerable only to those actors that finance their activities. Moreover, their scope within global health has mainly been limited to that of infectious disease, specifically "the big three"—tuberculosis, malaria, and HIV/ AIDS—and measurable outcomes. The next chapter explores what is meant by the big three, why they occupy such attention within global health before considering the realm of neglected health in Chapter 5.

4 The big three
Malaria, HIV/AIDS, and tuberculosis

- **Malaria**
- **HIV/AIDS**
- **Tuberculosis**
- **Conclusion**

Global health governance has been applied to a range of health concerns, illnesses, and biomedical research. Various health issues have been prioritized within the institutions that govern these concerns from tobacco in the World Health Organization (WHO) to maternal health within the World Bank and neglected disease within the Bill and Melinda Gates Foundation. What is similar between both old and new institutions involved in the governance of health and disease is the persistent interest and high profile accorded to the "big three" diseases: tuberculosis, malaria, and HIV/AIDS. Whilst some would argue that cancer, obesity, lifestyle choices, and tobacco-related diseases are the big health issues of the modern world, it is these three diseases that are met with policy frameworks and globally organized, large-scale financial assistance to tackle them. Whilst cancer research claims a high level of health financing in developed countries it does not undergo the same level of global coordination or policymaking; and whilst tobacco regulation is increasingly global through the Framework Convention on Tobacco Control (FCTC), it does not receive the same level of funding in seeing its fruition. The infectious aspect of tuberculosis and HIV, the global susceptibility to malaria, and the commitment between both the private and public sector marks these three diseases as exceptional.

"The big three" are linked by the following factors. First, they are most prevalent in developing countries, specifically sub-Saharan Africa and parts of South Asia. Second, infection with one often leads to susceptibility to another; this is specifically the case in the relationship between HIV/AIDS and tuberculosis. HIV infection can increase susceptibility to malaria, but HIV/AIDS per se does not drive the recent resurgence in malaria.[1] Third, they have all been internationally recognized as the three scourges on global health, and as such have become the central actors within a fund for global health, the Global Fund. Finally, they are tackled through global coordination frameworks at the state and local level. What sets them apart is the longevity of the diseases, the vectors of disease, and the ways in which they are addressed. Malaria and tuberculosis are said to be as old as mankind. In contrast, despite claims to AIDS existing as a form of "slim" disease in West Africa for the last 50 years, HIV was not formally identified until 1981. The governance of malaria and tuberculosis has evolved over centuries, yet it is the global nature of the governance of HIV/AIDS that has come to be applied to addressing these concerns. HIV/AIDS has received considerable political will and ensuing financial support in recent years, whereas efforts towards coordinated governance, will, and unity in approach to combating malaria and tuberculosis have waned. The governance of these three diseases has core similarities, the lessons of which can be applied to each other's governance.

This chapter outlines each of the big three diseases: what they are, when they were first identified, what measures and approaches to combating them have been taken, and who is setting the agenda. The chapter first looks at malaria, before focusing on HIV/AIDS and then tuberculosis. The chapter draws together the main themes of "the big three" to identify what they tell us about global health governance before beginning to think about what they exclude from the global health agenda in Chapter 5.

Malaria

According to the WHO, in 2008 there were 247 million cases of malaria, with an average of one million deaths per year.[2] The majority of these deaths are of children under five, mostly living in sub-Saharan Africa.[3] Malaria is a disease transmitted by mosquitoes, derived from the Italian word for "bad air." Mosquitoes carry the parasite plasmodium, which causes malaria. There are four different species of the parasite plasmodium: plasmodium vivax, plasmodium ovale, plasmodium malariae, and plasmodium falciparum. It is the falciparum species that is fatal and the most common parasite in sub-Saharan Africa and of greatest concern for efforts to combat the disease. Plasmodium falciparum is transmitted to humans by the infected female anopheles mosquito. The anopheles mosquito transmits the parasite when feeding on human blood; humans infected with the parasite can then infect non-infected anopheles mosquitoes, and hence the cycle continues. Plasmodium falciparum causes a tertian fever—where there is one day between outbursts of fever that last 2–3 days. This lethal form of malaria is evident when an individual suffers from shivering, high temperature and unbearable heat, stupor, fits and eventually a coma often leading to death. Indigenous adults in areas of high malarial prevalence can develop partial immunity in response to repeated infections, yet individuals are still susceptible to repeated attacks and related complications or other illness.[4]

Efforts to combat malaria have been notoriously difficult for a number of reasons, starting with the eradication of the vector of infection—the anopheles mosquito. Mosquitoes adapt and become resistant to insecticide, which in turn has negative side effects for local ecological systems, the environment, and human health. Water supply and drainage systems need to be effectively managed to prevent mosquitoes breeding, and be reactive to changes within the wider environment. Similar to the other two big diseases, malaria is intrinsically linked with poverty and under-development.[5] Countries where malaria is endemic tend to be poor, and countries where malaria has been eliminated have seen more rapid and sustained growth.[6] Similar to HIV/AIDS and tuberculosis, malaria leads to a decline in school attendance, reduction in work productivity, low birth weight in babies and severe maternal anaemia, and in some instances developmental abnormalities. It is this exceptionalism that makes its governance particularly complicated. This section looks at the governance of malaria in four stages: the identification and early discoveries in managing and combating the disease; the debate within the WHO over elimination and control of the 1950s and 1960s; the need for collaboration and a combination of horizontal and vertical strategies in the 1990s and the antecedents to Roll Back Malaria; and the quest for a vaccine and the future and lessons of global malaria governance.

Hope and the golden age: quinine and chloroquine

The first cases of malaria are hard to trace, with common understanding suggesting it has existed as long as humankind.[7] The plasmodium parasite is said to have evolved with humans, with the falciparum species adapting itself during the Neolithic period. There is evidence of malaria in the clinical writings of Hippocrates, and of its effects on the armies of ancient Rome and Greece, and their eventual decline.[8] Though there is some discrepancy over whether it pre-dates Columbus, malaria is understood to have spread from Africa to Europe to the Americas from the 1400s to 1600s with the growth in migration, exploration, and empire.[9] Regardless of the discrepancy between dates, the origins of malaria share several commonalities relevant to its governance today: its movement as a transborder infectious disease; its relationship to migration, climate, and changes in agriculture;[10] and the threat it poses to empire and the military strength of states. The relationship between malaria and empire provided the impetus for the need to treat, control, and eliminate malaria; however, this impetus was marred by a lack of knowledge as to a cause, treatment, or cure for the disease.

The governance of malaria is marked by seemingly divergent attempts at control and elimination. Control and elimination have been made possible by two important points in history: the discovery of the cinchona tree and Ronald Ross' discovery that mosquitoes transmit malaria. Quinine from the bark of the cinchona tree had been used to treat malaria for many years by the Incas. According to Knell, the 1600s saw Spanish priests bringing the "jesuit's powder" back to Europe to treat people with malaria.[11] However, it was not until 1749 that the bark of the "Peruvian fever tree," the cinchona, was globally recognized as offering a cure for malaria. Once the alkaloid—quinine—was extracted from the bark in 1820 the demand for cinchona soared. Capitalizing on this demand was "cockney trader" Charles Ledger, who conducted what Honigsbaum calls "the biggest robbery in history."[12] In 1861 Ledger sent his Peruvian servant Manuel Incra Macrami to collect the seeds of the cinchona tree; once collected Ledger sold the seeds on to Dutch traders, giving them a monopoly on the production and growth of quinine.[13]

Whilst quinine provided some degree of prevention and treatment for malaria, the cause of malaria was not identified until the "golden age" of microbiology with Ronald Ross' breakthrough in 1897. As Knell describes, Ross, a surgeon major in the Indian army, made the discovery that mosquitoes transmit malaria in Secunderabad, India, after focusing on the small brown, nocturnal anopheles mosquito instead of concentrating only on grey mosquitoes common during the day time.[14] Ross' finding was reported and confirmed by his friend and colleague Patrick Manson and Giovanni Battista Grassi who established the vector theory of disease by allowing mosquitoes to feed on volunteers (Manson's two sons) who became infected with the disease.[15] The discovery of quinine and the vector theory of disease gave those combating malaria the skills to do so. However, attempts at reduction during this stage were divided by overall reduction or elimination, and control or "risk" approaches that continue to make the governance of malaria problematic today.

The beginnings of the twentieth century saw a large demand for malaria control and its wider governance. Demand for control came from the general population, but with malaria primarily being a tropical disease it was located more predominantly in the global south, and thus less of a concern to policymakers in the north. The need for malaria control became a wider global health concern with the onset of war and empire building. The League of Nations Malaria Commission established at the end of the First World War advised states and public health workers on implementing prophylactic measures against malaria, and emphasized the continued need for studies exploring vectors and habits.[16] However, it was not until the end of the Second World War that the need for global malaria control and the necessary political will to do so became acute. Malaria had taken its toll on allied forces on the eastern front and in Africa, with more direct losses in Gallipoli being attributed to malaria than direct combat.[17] Quinine was seen to have a limited impact on treatment and prevention.

During the Second World War, the US military Committee on Medical Research began to develop anti-malaria and anti-viral drugs as part of a wider anti-malaria program.[18] The anti-malaria program existed alongside other high-profile and controversial projects of the time such as the radar program and the Manhattan Project.[19] This period of biomedical innovation by the US military saw the development of malarial chemotherapy as a wider strategy of the United States' preparation for war. By 1944 the first-line drug for malaria treatment—chloroquine—was at the point of readiness for civilian testing.[20] Chloroquine remains one of the principle means of treating malaria as a first-line drug in parts of sub-Saharan Africa. Combined, the loss of soldiers to malaria, recognition of the limits of quinine, and the political will to stimulate a new form of multilateralism and global order that prioritized health concerns gave the impetus for new means of combating and eliminating malaria and saw a boost on anti-malaria research and development on "an unprecedented scale."[21] It was in this context that the newly formed WHO called for the global eradication of malaria.

WHO and the quest for elimination

In 1955 the WHO launched its Malaria Eradication Program as one of its core flagship programs and a clear signal that malaria governance was moving away from control to elimination. The purpose of the program was to create a global infrastructure to generate and disseminate research, education, and expertise; coordinate national and international agencies in the pursuit of elimination; and help create national elimination programs within states through National Eradication Campaigns. The strategy was not based on the development of a vaccine as with its later success with smallpox, but the use of indoor spraying with dichloro-diphenyl-trichloroethane (DDT).[22] DDT would interrupt malaria transmission by attacking the mosquito vector. DDT was produced on a large scale, building on momentum on early successes of the campaign with over a hundred countries participating in the program by 1965 and slight declines in malaria prevalence.[23] According to Staples, drawing on contributions from the US government and UNICEF, the WHO provided insecticide and the necessary equipment to make eradication a reality. The campaign built upon the combination of political will, expert consensus, money, and staff confidence—the key elements of effective global health strategies.[24]

Despite building upon this winning combination of money, will, and expertise, elimination of malaria was only partly successful. Although not eliminated on a global basis, the program saw success in Europe, Russia, most of North America, parts of South America, the Caribbean, Japan, Singapore, and in several countries in the Middle East.[25] Eradication efforts became problematic with increased mosquito resistance to insecticides, inflation, and political instability.[26] By 1959 the WHO stopped subsidizing the cost of spraying personnel, and developing countries had diverted much of their health budgets towards malaria eradication, particularly towards DDT.[27] This was problematic as by the late 1960s there was increased evidence as to the negative side effects of DDT. DDT did severe ecological damage to insects, wildlife, and domestic pets.[28] People began to evade spraying their homes, concerned about the negative side effects.[29] In 1982 the US government stopped DDT production.[30] By 1969 the global campaign for eradication had ceased.

In 1969 the World Health Assembly (WHA) adopted a revised malaria strategy that balanced elimination and vector control with control of the organism. Elimination based on DDT spraying concentrated on vector control at the expense of blocking non-vector contact, drug prophylaxis, and the treatment of malaria.[31] The divide between what to control—the vector/organism, treatment/prevention—is a debate that underpins much contention within global health governance. The governance of malaria is no different, with policies ranging from general methods of species control, sanitation, medical care, primary health, and horizontal efforts to combat the disease, to more specific mosquito control through elimination, public health-based vertical interventions.[32] The limitations of elimination saw an increase in alternative methods of malaria control that adapts on environmental control, biological control, and personal protection.[33] Yet each element alone had only a limited impact; malaria governance requires a combined approach to control that adapts to the longevity and adaptability of the anopheles mosquito. The need for a balance between vertical and horizontal strategies seems quite obvious. However, as the governance of malaria from the 1950s to 1980s suggests, such a balance is not easily achieved.

Wilderness to Roll Back Malaria

The 1980s saw the WHO reorganize its malaria efforts once again to focus on the socio-economic aspects of the disease and emphasize eradication where feasible. Malaria during this period was not so much governed as ignored as health initiatives underwent public funding cuts in developing countries, and the focus returned to horizontal forms of health system strengthening. As Liese highlights, US funding for malaria declined from $120 million in 1989, to $10 million by 1990 during this period.[34] By January 1992, recognizing the need to recalibrate global efforts and draw attention to malaria, the WHO organized a ministerial conference. The outcome of the conference was four recommendations: i) "timely and adequate diagnosis and treatment of malarial disease provided as a right to all at-risk people"; ii) selective vector control that is cost-effective and sustainable; iii) rapid interventions facilitated by early-warning systems to detect risk; and iv) routine information systems to monitor malaria situations.[35] These recommendations depended on local support systems to be developed in the context of a multisectoral approach to malaria control that involved multiple actors in the delivery of services and information systems, and the coordination of research activities. Multisectoralism would combine the public sector, the private non-profit sector, the private commercial sector, and the "private unofficial or informal sector," that is, communities and families[36] to help overcome problems of financial resources, flexibility, and lack of information, treatment, and monitoring of malaria at the community level.

Towards the end of the 1990s there was general consensus as to the effective tools, mechanisms, and responsibilities for tackling malaria. Prevention could be achieved through a combination of insecticide bed nets, indoor spraying, swamp drainage and destruction of mosquito larvae, and intermittent preventive treatment for pregnant women.

Resistance to chloroquine and sulfadoxine-pyrimethamine meant that treatment would best be met through artemsinin combination therapy— ACT. Where resources are tight, chloroquine would still be used as a first-line drug, a typical problem of global health governance. The implementation of these strategies would depend on financial support from international donors, coordination by the WHO and national Ministries of Health, primary healthcare delivery at the community level, combined research, and effective monitoring and implementation systems by public and private bodies. It was in this context that the WHO, United Nations Children's Fund (UNICEF), United Nations Development Programme (UNDP), and the World Bank launched the global campaign to Roll Back Malaria.

The objective of Roll Back Malaria was to halve the burden of malaria over 10 years, from its official launch date in 2000 to 2010. The project was a joint initiative between the WHO, World Bank, UNICEF, UNDP, donors, non-governmental organizations (NGOs), academia, and malaria endemic countries. In practice, the program was housed within the WHO, but was subject to much influence from the World Bank and UNICEF in particular. The focus on the project was the reinforcement and strengthening of health systems through global partnerships and support networks, support to impact indicators, national governance, and local community involvement to improve incidence reporting, feedback, and data collection. Operation and design of the project would be country-specific, cost-effective, and engage in partnerships to fulfill state objectives. The purpose of this was to overcome challenges in monitoring, shortages, and limitations within healthcare infrastructures, access to medicine and bed nets, and progress in insecticide and vaccine development.

Roll Back Malaria proved to be successful in the following ways. First it galvanized political support and financial commitment towards malaria not seen since the drive for elimination of the 1950s. For example, by 2004, the Bill and Melinda Gates Foundation had pledged $268 million for vaccines, new drugs, and pesticides and the Bush administration $1.2 billion.[37] The Gates Foundation's Global Malaria Action Plan, developed in accordance and within the context of Roll Back Malaria, prioritizes "aggressive control," "progressive elimination," and research into better drugs, insecticides, diagnostics, and vaccines.[38] This commitment has been met with the formation of a Malaria Elimination Group by the Global Health Group at the University of California[39] and renewed efforts and research into finding a vaccine. Political commitment has been seen within states where malaria is endemic, and with the growth in private actors raising funds and implementing programs. Such support translated into efforts to improve health systems in developing countries. Combined with efforts towards combating HIV/AIDS and tuberculosis, the project highlighted the need for a global fund to combat these three diseases within an operational multisectoral structure supported by bilateral and multilateral funding strategies.

Long-term support and results from Roll Back Malaria were, however, limited by common problems of resources to implement the most effective methods of prevention and treatment, and doubt over the ability to reach the target established in 1998. Malaria rates have increased and the WHO "has accumulated an expansive list of missed opportunities and dismal failures."[40] In terms of treatment, the cost of ACT led to the widespread production and consumption of counterfeit drugs, often sold and self-prescribed on the black market.[41] Moreover, donors in some cases were unwilling to support the cost of ACT as it is 10 times more expensive than chloroquine. For example, when seeking aid from the Global Fund to support ACT interventions, governments "are forcefully pressured out of it by governments such as the USA, whose aid officials say that ACT is too expensive and not ready for prime time."[42] Institutions such as the WHO and Global Fund have to align with such approaches despite acknowledging the greater success of ACT as a means of maintaining funding. Hence, even where medical knowledge and advances exist, the funds and necessary will to support such "innovation" do not exist.

The central element of Roll Back Malaria—health system strengthening—suffered from the familiar bottlenecks, inadequate staffing, lack of equipment, provision of basic services, and procurement and support that continue to plague and undermine global health interventions. The World Bank launched a "Booster Programme for Malaria Control" in 2005 to address these issues through the provision of additional technical support and the development of long-term public–private partnerships (PPPs) to stimulate sustainable interventions against malaria.[43] Developing the work of the Bank in this regard, the Global Fund has since invested considerable sums of money towards horizontal health system strengthening to overcome these problems. There are tangible results with the increased opening of healthcare centers and more local-centered interventions, yet the long-term effects and sustainability of these efforts are yet to be seen. A further problem has been that despite the general agreement towards a global strategy that is nationally based, confusions over accepted measures of progress and what constitutes impact remain unresolved.[44] Interventions rely on political stability, with minimal strategies that allow for civil unrest or warfare that lead to instability and disruption to health systems.[45]

Common to most problems with global health interventions, the blame for the lack of impact on the reversal of malaria has been placed on states and failures of national health systems. However, these failures overlook the institutional problems and leadership squabbles endemic to organizations at the center of global health governance. Roll Back Malaria was introduced as a key element of Gro Harlem Brundtland's leadership of the WHO. Brundtland "pledged to reverse the despondency towards malaria;"[46] however, the priority accorded to malaria and its specialist partnerships separated it from the wider structures and staff of the WHO. As the brief history of the WHO in Chapter 2 suggests, prioritizing specific health concerns and identifying them as somewhat separate to the day-to-day activities of the WHO often leads to staff inertia, low morale, and resentment towards these issues. The real problem for combating malaria, however, has been the nature of peaks and shortfalls of money.[47] This problem has been in part addressed by the formation of the Global Fund (see Chapter 3); however, replenishment of the Fund has started to wane and malaria continues to take a backseat to funding initiatives for HIV/AIDS. Whilst Roll Back Malaria and the Global Fund led to a boost in attention towards malaria, there is evidence to suggest that 2010–20 will be marked by a shortfall in political will and financial support.

Search for a vaccine and new forms of collaborative research

The one long-term objective that has undergone renewed interest within global health governance has been the search for a malaria vaccine. Funding for research and development of a malaria vaccine reached $60–70 million in 2004[48] and recently doubled as part of the Bill and Melinda Gates Foundation pledge of $168 million to fund PATH's anti-malaria vaccine development in 2008. The development of a malaria vaccine poses two central questions: who funds the resource? And how is the resource evenly distributed? Should a vaccine be developed it would be subject to patent allowing the drug to be sold at a higher rate to recoup the cost of research and development. The problem with a vaccine would be how those living in countries where malaria is endemic can afford to pay for it. The development and problems of potential distribution of vaccines has seen the development of specific forms of PPPs, product development public–private partnerships—PDPPPs (!)—such as Medicines for Malaria Venture and the Malaria Vaccine Initiative. As Chapter 3 highlighted, these partnerships tend to be not for profit, and have the over-arching purpose of generating greater collaboration between public and private sectors to advance both basic and applied research to develop new products for global health in developing countries.[49]

These partnerships are a vital part to the mechanisms and operations of global health governance, and are often cited as one of the core forms of innovation, principally in reference to strategies against malaria and tuberculosis. They have in part been effective, in acknowledging and bringing these problems into the public and private domain of policymaking, and have made minor inroads in drug pricing in developing countries. Moreover, they have facilitated an upsurge in interest in the prospect of a malaria vaccine that contrasts sharply with the lack of interest or funds in the 1970s and 1980s. However, despite progress in partnership, there remains little resolution to the problem of profit and what constitutes equitable distribution, antimalarial drugs continue to be an unattractive investment for pharmaceutical companies,[50] and hence there is currently little sight of a malaria vaccine.

Governing malaria

The failure to control malaria has been attributed to several factors: i) the shifting emphasis between control and elimination; ii) the lack of funds to support integrated intervention strategies; iii) the cost of patent and generic drugs, chloroquine, and ART; and iv) the complexity of the disease and its relationship to socio-economic and environmental change. Efforts to govern malaria suggest the following about global health governance. Health threats to militaries and state security generate political will and financial investment in addressing the causes of disease and innovation and research. Thus diseases such as malaria have an intrinsic relationship to security. Financing for diseases such as malaria shows a pattern of peaks and troughs, that ultimately undermines any progress made during peak funding times. To address global health challenges, consistent and sustained funding is required. New institutional arrangements and initiatives can have initial positive impact; yet such impact is measured against their ability to adapt to changes in disease and the wider global political economy. There is an argument that should current efforts to combat malaria prove unsuccessful, responsibility will not only be attributed to states and the WHO but will be apportioned to the range of actors involved in the development and delivery of anti-malaria strategies. For malaria interventions to be effective, donors as well as the coordinators and hosts of anti-malaria strategies need to be held to account. This issue of accountability and transparency is pertinent to the successful combat of "the big 3" diseases specifically, as the next section on the governance of HIV/AIDS will show.

HIV/AIDS

Since its formal recognition in 1981, HIV/AIDS has come to constitute the most recognized, highly funded and contested global health issue. Its "exceptional" nature and the complexity surrounding the stigma, funding, and socio-economic determinants of the disease have made its governance and position in global health unique. According to WHO/ UNAIDS data at the time of press, there are 33 million people living with HIV/AIDS in the world, 22 million of whom live in sub-Saharan Africa.[51] Human Immune Deficiency Virus, most commonly referred to as HIV, is the virus that causes Acquired Immune Deficiency Syndrome—AIDS. HIV, is a "lentivirus" that develops over a long period of time, often going unnoticed to those first infected. Infection occurs when the virus enters the body through one of the following means: i) sexual transmission via unprotected anal or vaginal intercourse, and in some instances oral sex in cases where individuals have gum disease/ abrasions in their mouth; ii) blood and blood products; iii) intravenous drug use and the sharing of unclean needles; and iv) mother to child transmission. The most common mode of transmission is sexual intercourse. Once the virus enters the human body it attaches itself to two types of host cell—predominantly CD4 cells, but also immune cells called macrophages—the virus then penetrates the cell wall, copies the cell's DNA, and thus becomes undetectable to the body's immune system.[52] The virus then reproduces itself, destroying the host CD4 cell and going on to infect more cells. This is called "the window period" where the virus mutates and the body produces more antibodies to combat infection. During this period the person is highly infectious, but the virus often goes undetected.[53] This period can last either many weeks or many months, until the "incubation stage" wherein the virus kills immune cells at a rate quicker than they can be replaced.[54] Once a person's CD4 count falls below 200 per microliter of blood (an average "healthy" person has 1,200 cells per microliter) they are more susceptible to opportunistic infection and are said to have AIDS.

HIV/AIDS was first recognized among gay men in the United States and Western Europe in the late 1970s–early 1980s, when men were mysteriously dying of a slimming disease or "gay cancer" that targeted their immune system. The association with gay men led to the name gay-related immune deficiency syndrome (GRID) associated with Kaposi's sarcoma. It was not until wider recognition of the disease among hemophiliacs, injecting drug users, and mothers who used drugs in the early 1980s that, the disease was identified with non-homosexual men and women. The disease was subsequently renamed Acquired

Immune Deficiency Syndrome (AIDS).[55] By 1981 AIDS was acknowledged as a worldwide phenomenon with incidence and death from the disease being identified in North America, Europe, Australia, Latin America, and parts of South and East Africa. During this time, there was no treatment or cure for AIDS or effective prevention strategies as the cause of AIDS was still unknown.

In 1983 Luc Montagnier of the Pasteur Institute discovered and identified HIV-1 as the cause of AIDS. The rarer form of the virus, HIV-2 that is slower acting, more difficult to transmit, and predominantly found in West Africa, was not identified until 1985.[56] Similar to tuberculosis, Montagnier's claims to discovery were met with controversy as Robert Gallo of the US National Institutes of Health's National Cancer Institute claimed to have discovered the virus first. In 1992, Montagnier was formally recognized as discovering the virus, but both are commonly referred to as having co-discovered HIV. The source of HIV remains contentious and often associated with wild conspiracy theories as to its origin. The most generally accepted explanation is that it crossed the species barrier from the simian immunodeficiency virus found in monkeys in Africa to humans. According to Barnett and Whiteside, how it crossed this barrier can be explained by the following competing theories: i) bush meat; ii) contaminated polio vaccine used in 1950s vaccine trials; iii) ritual behavior, for example, use of monkey blood in ceremony; or iv) the use of contaminated needles.[57]

The mode of transmission and lifecycle of the virus make HIV/AIDS difficult to govern as actors within global health governance often lack or are in disagreement as to the most effective tools to prevent and treat the disease. The way in which HIV mutates and is hard to recognize in the "window period" of infection makes its treatment difficult. The main mode of transmission—sexual intercourse—should make prevention easy through education about safe sex. However, sex and sexuality has become a difficult area for public policy to address as it affects the traditionally closed-off sphere of the family, the personal or the private. Conspiracy as to whether HIV causes AIDS, where HIV comes from, and stigma surrounding the "gay" or "dirty" nature of the disease makes efforts to govern an effective response difficult and complex. Compounding these factors is the widespread recognition that HIV/AIDS is both driven by and is a driver of socio-economic inequality and poverty.[58] HIV/AIDS infects and affects women disproportionately to men. Women are more susceptible to HIV infection due to not only physiological factors but their gender role in societies with high HIV prevalence.[59] In addition, it is women who fulfill the role of carer for ill family members and neighbors, and adoptive roles for orphans and vulnerable children. Girls are more likely to leave school before boys to care for their sick parents and fulfill household roles; and engage in transactional sex with older men.[60] Combined these factors make HIV/AIDS an "exceptional" health issue, that requires a complex, multi-faceted response that extends beyond solely health initiatives.

The initial response: stigma and denial

The initial response to HIV/AIDS was stigma and denial. Care for the sick and prevention activities were conducted by self-organized support groups among gay communities in North America and Europe, and local communities in less developed countries. State responses to the epidemic were slow and not forthcoming, with states acting in denial as to the threat of the virus, or their responsibility in doing anything about it. This can be seen throughout the world from Ronald Reagan in the United States, Margaret Thatcher in the United Kingdom, to Thabo Mbeki in South Africa.[61] There were slight exceptions to this level of state involvement, with the Brazilian government taking the lead in addressing the problem early on. However, part of the Brazilian government's willingness to do so stemmed from wider pressure from proactive and responsive civil society actors. The stigma and denial that resulted in silence surrounding the initial stages of the epidemic, did little to curb its spread throughout populations, as the reach of education, care, and treatment programs was severely curtailed by the lack of central government organization. Part of the stigma and denial arose out of the labeling of HIV/AIDS as a "gay disease" that stimulated wider feelings of homophobia and questions as to the role of the family, and the state in intervening in family or the "personal" life of its citizens. Simply put states lacked the political will or interest in combating the disease. Contributing to the lack of such political will was the cost of responding to the epidemic. This cost not only refers to the core areas of care, treatment, support, and prevention but extended to funding of biomedical, epidemiological, and sociological research into the determinants of the disease and treatment methods to combat it. Confusion as to the nature of epidemics, stigmatization of those people who were seen to be infected with the disease, and a lack of understanding as to how to treat and combat it set a precedent of confusion and denial that ultimately led to state silence and inactivity.

This inactivity within the state set several precedents for the future of the global response to the epidemic. First, that political will in both developed and developing countries is at a minimum when it comes to addressing HIV/AIDS. Second, from the outset HIV/AIDS has been framed as a complex or somehow exceptional disease that makes its treatment and prevention difficult. Third, community interventions based on a must-do attitude underpin the global HIV/AIDS response, and have acted as a tool of advocacy in getting states and intergovernmental organizations to recognize the problem and respond to their views and knowledge. Fourth, the lifespan of the virus and the personal nature of the disease have made the tools in which to combat it difficult to ascertain and subject to political manipulation. As with malaria and tuberculosis, HIV/AIDS suffers from similar problems of treatment through chemotherapy, the most appropriate prevention strategies, the need for wider investment in the search for a vaccine, problems with data, and whether vertical or horizontal programs should be pursued. However, where HIV/AIDS differs from malaria and tuberculosis is the sheer level of funding and multiple actors involved in combating it. Since the 1990s, the response to HIV/AIDS has become a global response that sought to rectify the stigma, denial, and silence that overshadowed any interventions in the early stages of the epidemic.

WHO—UNAIDS—to everyone

Recognition of HIV/AIDS as a global pandemic that demonstrated the interconnectedness and interdependent nature of states led to a shift from state-based interventions to intergovernmental action. At the core of initial global efforts to govern the disease was the WHO and the Global Programme on HIV/AIDS (GPA). The WHO was officially recognized by the UN as the lead agency in combating HIV/AIDS through 1987 and 1988 UN Economic and Social Council (ECOSOC) resolutions, highlighting the need for a lead agency to gain donor support and leadership in response to the pandemic. In its initial stages, HIV/AIDS fell under the remit of the Division of Communicable Diseases as part of the WHO's "Global Strategy for Prevention and Control of AIDS."[62] This strategy provided the underpinnings for what was to become the GPA. According to Lisk, formerly established in 1987, the GPA was created out of the need to mobilize resources for HIV/AIDS as a global pandemic that was having severe effects on the health and development of populations, specifically within sub-Saharan Africa.[63] Under the Directorship of Jonathan Mann, the GPA adopted a rights-based approach to HIV/AIDS, that underpinned the need to consider the socio-economic causes and outcomes of the disease and the exceptional, or non-health-specific element to combating it. For its part, the GPA can be considered a success in its ability to bring HIV/AIDS to the attention of member states of the UN and developing countries. It raised the profile of HIV/AIDS, and in so doing began to secure large-scale multilateral and bilateral funding to help support government systems. However, in many ways the GPA was set up to fail from the outset. It was formed six years after the discovery of HIV, and had to play catch-up in instigating biomedical research, incentivizing government responses, measuring the scale of the pandemic, and identifying treatment and prevention strategies. These issues were combined with an organization that was stalwart in positioning its primary concern as health and better health outcomes for all, with little assessment or integration as to how the role of globalization and changes in the global political economy affected such outcomes. This tension led to an inability to change or reverse the trajectory in which the WHO was set.

The WHO was the obvious choice in which to place a global program for combating HIV/AIDS; however, the above factors and institutional problems led to its ultimate demise. As Lisk highlights, the emphasis of the new director general of the WHO, Hiroshi Nakajima, in 1988 was towards decentralizing the operations of the GPA, reorienting its work more towards health outcomes, and reining in the personal leadership of Mann.[64] This led to the establishment of a general management committee and external review committee to assess the role of the GPA in 1989.[65] In the short term this led to the resignation of the charismatic Mann in 1990. In the long term it led to a reappraisal of the global strategy for governing HIV/AIDS. This reappraisal renewed the emphasis on the rights-based approach taken by the GPA, but crucially broadened the governance structure in which this could be achieved through more co-sponsorship and multiple participating actors with any overarching structure performing a coordinating role.[66] Between the WHO and UN the "Task Force on HIV/AIDS coordination" was established as a means of implementing such coordination and co-sponsorship structures. The result of this was the formation of UNAIDS, that began to take shape in 1995, but formally came into operation in January 1996 under the leadership of Peter Piot. The formation of UNAIDS marked the start of the WHO's declining role in HIV/AIDS interventions. The WHO maintains a role in country support and health system strengthening, and the gathering of data, yet this role has since been sidelined by a multitude of other actors, with much greater funds, expertise, and flexibility. The WHO's most recent flagship program—the 3by5 initiative—to get 3 million people on antiretroviral treatment by 2005, was widely seen as being of only limited success. As such, the WHO has now come to perform a side role in the governance of HIV/AIDS.

As with its initial mandate, the main function of UNAIDS is to coordinate the operations of its UN co-sponsors—UN High Commission for Refugees (UNHCR), UNICEF, WHO, World Bank, International Labour Organization (ILO), UN Office on Drugs and Crime (UNODC), UNDP, UN Educational, Scientific and Cultural Organization (UNESCO), and UNFPA—in efforts to combat HIV/AIDS. UNAIDS has the role of collection and dissemination of epidemiological data on the state of the epidemic; guidance and support to governments as to how to effectively implement HIV/AIDS strategies and coordinate with donors; maintaining the high profile of HIV/AIDS on the global policy agenda as well as giving a voice to contentious issues such as men who have sex with men; and providing general leadership, guidance, and performing an "honest broker" role between co-sponsors and donors. Crucially, UNAIDS is not a funding body or a donor, despite some of its co-sponsors performing such a function. Under Peter Piot's leadership (1996–2008) UNAIDS has to a degree succeeded where the GPA failed in sustaining unprecedented levels of financial support and political will in combating HIV/AIDS. It has held its position as an honest broker and maintained the exceptional nature of the disease. It has succeeded in highlighting issues of controversy, and encouraging states with high HIV/AIDS prevalence rates to take responsibility for their epidemics. Importantly, it has kept its relevance as the central coordinating body of HIV/AIDS despite a huge growth in actors and funding streams from both the public and private sector operating at multiple levels of governance. However, since Piot's departure and the appointment of Michel Sidibe, the role of UNAIDS remains but its activities and operations to maintain relevance have become fuzzy. Since Sidibe's appointment, UNAIDS appears to have reasserted the role of rights in governing HIV/AIDS and promoting the need to combat the prevention of mother to child transmission as an achievable aim. As Chapter 6 will highlight, this is strategic in keeping HIV/AIDS on the global health agenda as funding shifts towards maternal and child health. However, UNAIDS' leadership role is increasingly second to that of four donors in the governance of HIV/AIDS: the World Bank, the Global Fund, PEPFAR, and the Bill and Melinda Gates Foundation.

As a co-sponsor of UNAIDS, the World Bank has played a prominent role in the governance of HIV/AIDS since the 1990s. Beyond UNAIDS, the World Bank has carved out a role within the governance of HIV/AIDS as the agenda setter of strategies to combat the epidemic since the turn of the century through its Multi-Country AIDS Program and the multisectoral agenda it pursued.[67] This program established the need for a multi-sectoral approach to HIV/AIDS that involves all aspects of the private, public, state, non-state, and international community in combating HIV/AIDS. The program fulfilled such a need by establishing in-country systems that have since rivaled Ministries of Health for ownership of an individual country's HIV/AIDS agenda, and precipitated an upsurge in community-level civil society activity throughout sub-Saharan Africa.[68] UNAIDS and the Global Fund have since come to mirror the strategies implemented and promoted by the bank in this regard[69] through an emphasis on multisectoralism as the central model for HIV/AIDS intervention, and the role of central planning and coordination strategies based on loose country ownership and donor support.

As with tuberculosis and malaria, the introduction of the Global Fund in 2000 led to a widespread reassessment of global health funding and consolidated the global political will and need for funds to combat shared problems of global health. The Global Fund has changed the landscape of HIV/AIDS financing by generating unprecedented sums of money and delivering them through a decentralized model. The fund has been instrumental in broader uptake of anti-retroviral treatment across sub-Saharan Africa, and the framing of country-owned and country-based agendas. However, beyond providing a deliberative function by including non-state actors in decision-making processes, the Global Fund has done very little to alter the governance of HIV/AIDS, beyond re-enforcing the structures of the World Bank and UNAIDS.[70]

The sheer scale of funding given to infectious diseases by the Bill and Melinda Gates Foundation has led to it occupying a central role in the governance of HIV/AIDS. The foundation has emphasized the scientific and innovative component of governing HIV/AIDS and similar to the Bank and Global Fund has channeled money to non-state actors, though slightly different in its preference for larger, US or Western European INGOs, and the private sector.[71] Similar to the Global Fund, the foundation has established new forms of PPP aimed at offering broader perspectives and approaches to governing HIV/AIDS, and securing funds to do so. One key example of such PPPs has been the Global Alliance for Vaccines and Immunisation (GAVI) (see Chapter 3).

Announced as part of George W. Bush's 28 January 2003 State of the Union address, the US President's Emergency Plan for AIDS Relief (PEPFAR) is a bilateral funding program of the US government. Launched just after the MAP, PEPFAR was initially a US$15 billion five-year strategy that would integrate care, treatment, and prevention programs across the world, with a focus upon rapid disbursement and results. That is, large commitments to the provision of ART and strengthening Ministry of Health capacity. PEPFAR has since been renewed in 2008 with a pledge of US$48 billion to continue targeting HIV/AIDS, malaria, and tuberculosis over five years. The shifting focus on treatment and a scaling up of ART under PEPFAR have resulted in a shift away from holistic approaches to prevention. For some, the financial capacity alone has led the United States to subsequently dominate HIV/AIDS efforts at the risk of UN marginalization. To stress its relevance, the UN must now align its interests and activities within a United States-led framework.[72] The arrival of PEPFAR has seen an increasing shift towards a biomedical and security discourse. The rising dominance of the health agenda has in part been pushed by for-profit healthcare providers, pharmaceutical companies, trends in biotechnology and health insurance providers.[73] The future of PEPFAR beyond 2013 is questionable; however, it was an intrinsic player in generating funds for HIV/AIDS and developing a results-oriented framework that permeates wider policies of the United States Agency for International Development (USAID) and philanthropic foundations.

Beyond these four main donors, bilateral donors have their own projects, and offer regular contributions to in-country basket funding mechanisms. These basket funds tend to be managed by government agencies; nominally the National AIDS Councils. National AIDS Councils provide a leadership and coordination role or the HIV/AIDS response within a state. They draw up national strategic plans alongside the private sector, civil society, and donor partnership groups, and in some cases administer donor funds to local community groups. These councils target the multisectoral element of intervention, whereas the ministries of health focus on the biomedical side and health system strengthening. If these government agencies are the central focus of coordination and management, implementation of services is decentralized to District and Provincial AIDS Councils, as well as national and INGOs, the private sector, and local community groups. The focus of HIV/AIDS governance has primarily been at the state level, with international organizations, donors, and civil society groups working towards state ownership, transparency, and accountability within the process. Multisectoral participation is seen by the international community as central to the achievement of these objectives. However, in practice multisectoral participation, country ownership, and donor coordination have been problematic. National AIDS Councils and similar government bodies tend to be over-run with donor demands and preferences, strategic plans have to align with those priority areas international donors are willing to support, and coordination between intergovernmental and governmental donor agencies tend to descend into turf war over mandate and claims to success.[74] A fundamental problem within this has been the uneasy relationship between the state and civil society.

As the history of the governance of HIV/AIDS suggests, civil society and transnational advocacy campaigns have been key components in raising the profile of the disease and demanding public responses to the global pandemic. Civil society-led campaigns have ensured that HIV/AIDS remains an exceptional disease in regards to the attention it receives, the need for understanding not stigma, and rights-based strategies. Funding towards HIV/AIDS since 2000 has emphasized the need for community-based interventions and multisectoral participation. This has seen a rise in the sheer number of civil society groups working to address the disease as well as the variety of type. As Chapter 3 demonstrated, civil society working on global health issues is no longer limited to large INGOs, but is characterized by small community groups, individuals, and highly organized national NGOs, usually founded and led by people living with HIV. The positive result of this has been widespread participation in HIV/AIDS governance, that breaks stigma, delivers community-responsive programs, and a decentralization of responsibility. However, such involvement in delivery at the community level has failed to translate to decision-making at the national and global level. Civil society engagement within centers of decision-making remains tokenistic and dominated by larger national and international NGOs. Moreover, much community activity has been motivated by the money available for HIV/AIDS-related activities, creating a market for the delivery of services based on economic gain rather than rights.[75]

Crisis and the future—is HIV/AIDS too exceptional?

HIV/AIDS governance is donor-directed, not necessarily by those with the most money, but those with close relationships to the state and wider processes of global HIV/AIDS governance. It is underpinned by a contention over biomedical or multisectoral approaches to interventions that reflect the longstanding debate over vertical and horizontal strategies within global health governance. Multisectoralism has generated an increase in actors responding to HIV/AIDS at the local, community, state, international, and regional levels. The result of this is the need for more coordination and articulation as to what the goals of such governance mechanisms are. The presence of multiple actors and funding streams fosters competition, overlap, and a lack of direction to how governance unfolds. Contrary to malaria and tuberculosis, the WHO has a marginal role to play and has struggled to find its mandate for HIV/AIDS since the demise of the GPA. In broadening governance beyond the WHO, actors involved in HIV/AIDS governance have been effective in gaining much needed political will and the money that comes with it. This in itself is an exceptional feat. The governance of HIV/AIDS can thus be characterized as disaggregated and multisectoral, with high levels of financial support and leadership through coordination. The governance of HIV/AIDS has become so broad that it is difficult to identify what is being governed and the purpose of governance, whether that be health, social behavior, security, or the wider problem of socio-economic development.

The 2008 global credit crunch and the exceptional nature of HIV/AIDS has led many public health and development workers, policymakers, and researchers to suggest that spending towards the disease should be reinvested to other health and development problems. For many the 10-year splurge on HIV/AIDS that has occurred since 2000 cannot be sustained, and the outcome to such spending and activity is hard to measure. To sustain such funding, the governance of HIV/AIDS has continued to rely on the need for innovation in introducing new ideas and concepts to receive funds and attention as a means of proving progress. However, areas of innovation, for example, efforts to produce a vaccine, have shown little return on investment. Worse, the problems of stigma, denial, and silence seen at the outset of the HIV/AIDS pandemic have not gone away and in some areas are as a greater problem as they were in the 1980s.

Some progress has been made in combating HIV/AIDS. Data in 2009 suggest that 33 million people are living with HIV/AIDS around the world, rather than the 40 million thought previously. More people have access to medicines and methods of prevention than before. However, the vast majority of people living with HIV do not have access to treatment, and people living in countries with high levels of HIV prevalence and incidence remain unaware of basic methods of prevention. Socio-economic inequalities and stigma remain pertinent. Hence, despite an improvement in health structures, quality and affordability of drugs, and greater awareness, the problem and threat of HIV/AIDS remains. The governance of HIV/AIDS rests on funding, hence any future success in combating the disease will depend on sustaining the unprecedented levels of funds aimed at combating the disease seen over the last 10 years.

Tuberculosis

Tuberculosis remains a central issue of global concern despite the long-term identification of the cause of infection, drugs for treatment, and an available vaccine. In this sense tuberculosis differs significantly from HIV/AIDS and malaria. However, HIV/AIDS, climate change and sustained poor standards of living have led to resurgence in tuberculosis in developing countries, and to a certain extent, developed countries. Tuberculosis differs from the governance of HIV/AIDS and malaria as it has introduced the most direct form of governance of surveillance and observation of bodies and human activity through the WHO's directly observed treatment, short-term (DOTS) recommendations, and contrary to HIV/AIDS and malaria has commonly agreed upon strategies by which to implement global interventions through local community interaction. Tuberculosis can be controlled by prevention methods such as vaccination and isolation, and treated through drug combination.[76] What the governance of tuberculosis has often been seen to lack has been the political will necessary to implement effective strategies. Standalone interventions have been led by the creaking WHO with other political support or will arising from combining tuberculosis with treatment for HIV. This section explores the following: i) what tuberculosis is, and its basic epidemiology; ii) the historical context to its governance and the emergence of the tools for effective tuberculosis control; iii) how tuberculosis is addressed and the actors at the center of its governance; and iv) the DOTS strategy and the future of tuberculosis interventions.

What is tuberculosis and why does it matter to global health governance?

Tuberculosis is an infectious disease, transmitted either by person to person via infected sputum and inhalation to the respiratory system—mycobacterium tuberculosis, or through human consumption of animal products infected with the disease—mycobacterium bovis. Measures to prevent mycobacterium bovis through pasteurization of milk, financial concessions to farmers, and control standards have seen a decline and effective monitor of this strain of tuberculosis throughout the world.[77] The governance of tuberculosis tends to focus on mycobacterium tuberculosis, which is the central focus of this section. Tuberculosis is caused by the organism tubercle bacilli, a rod-shaped bacterium belonging to the mycobacteriacae type of microorganisms that use oxygen to grow.[78] A person becomes infected when they inhale airborne tuberculosis. However, inhalation only leads to infection where the bacteria are more powerful than a person's immune system; hence if someone is ill or their immune system is weak they are more susceptible. This accounts for the difference between tuberculosis infection, and active tuberculosis. Whilst a third of the world's population is infected with the tuberculosis bacilli, only a tenth of this will become sick with active tuberculosis.[79] The problem with treating tuberculosis is similar to malaria and HIV in that it is adaptable and resistant to treatment and has a complex timetable, from infection to when symptoms are identified, hence the need for combined and sustained treatment.[80]

Tuberculosis matters to global health governance because of its recent resurgence and potential threat to both developed and developing countries. In 2005 there were 8.8 million new cases of tuberculosis, the majority of which were the fatal form of pulmonary tuberculosis;[81] by 2008 there were 9.4 million cases. However, recent data suggest global incidence of tuberculosis is slowly falling.[82] According to Dye and Borgdorff, the highest rate of fatality is in Africa, but the highest rate of incidence is in countries with large and growing populations such as India, China, Indonesia, and Pakistan.[83] Incidence is increasing in sub-Saharan Africa and parts of eastern Europe, predominantly countries of the ex-Soviet Union, and is declining in West and Central Europe, North America, Latin America, the Middle East, and South East Asia. Contrary to HIV/AIDS which is increasingly seen as a feminized disease, tuberculosis disproportionately affects men.[84] Tuberculosis is often described as a social disease because of its relationship to social environment such as poor living conditions.[85] Hence specific groups such as the elderly, homeless people, prison inmates, and those susceptible to occupational risk tend to be seen as "high risk" to infection.[86] Despite incidence rates slowly declining globally and a relatively high level of treatment success, tuberculosis highlights the relationship between health and socio-economic inequality and poverty. Tuberculosis "is the leading killer of people with HIV"[87] and hence affects people in developing countries in their young productive years of ages 15–35, driving the poverty cycle between health and productivity.

Similar to malaria, tuberculosis is not a new disease. Tuberculosis was referred to as "phthisis" in Ancient Greece and Rome, "consumption" in the medieval and renaissance period, and "the white plague" in the nineteenth century.[88] Tuberculosis has remained a constant threat throughout history, yet similar to modern times, has often been overlooked or sidelined by other "bigger plagues" such as smallpox and leprosy[89] and most recently, HIV. As such, a search for the treatment and cause of tuberculosis was at its most acute in the nineteenth century during the industrial revolution when an increase in poor living conditions, anxiety, urbanization, poor diet, and alcohol consumption saw a growth in incidence of active tuberculosis. Various herbal remedies such as "Umckaloabo" south African plant and faith cure "secret remedies"[90] were rumored and experimented with, but any form of drug treatment was initially not forthcoming. Treatment has ranged from extended stays in sanatoria, health tourism, bloodletting, and advanced drug treatment to vaccination. In general, treatment for tuberculosis can be defined by the following categories: the fresh air and sanitary movement; the chemotherapy era; and the emergence of DOTS.

Fresh air and the sanatoria movement

From ancient Greece to the end of the nineteenth century, fresh air was the dominant method of treating tuberculosis. Greek philosophers such as Plato and Aristotle expressed pity for those afflicted with tuberculosis but thought care was a waste of time and a burden to the state, whereas Hippocrates recommended clean air as the most simple and best means of treating the disease.[91] During the late nineteenth century the increased incidence was met with the widespread introduction of private sanatoria run by religious organizations and workhouses. The purpose of this was to provide a place where "consumptives" would have space to rest, take in fresh air, and be free from the stress and anxiety of work and family commitments.[92] Doctors highlighted the need for patients to "will" themselves to get better, and focusing on the "inner man" in regards to mental strength and encouragement through letter writing, stamp collecting, reading, and sedate game playing, this would all assist patients in "taking the cure."[93] Smoking was permitted in some cases "provide it doesn't make you cough" and alcohol was not seen to "harm the cure, but in moderation"; the only thing that was seen to do the most harm was "romance" or external visitors.[94] Beyond fresh air, some sanatoria introduced forms of surgical interventions for treating tuberculosis. These treatments ranged from the cutting of chest adhesions, re-sectioning of the ribs and vertebrae to remove lesions from the lungs[95] and purification through bloodletting,[96] to the more common pneumothorax, or lung collapse of the 1920s and 1930s. The emergence of sanatoria saw a growth in health tourism and migration, as people moved to areas of fresh air, or to rural settings.

Sanatoria and the need to provide care for the workforce as a means of securing productivity and growth at a time of industrial expansion led to a wider recognition of the role of public health authorities in the prevention and treatment of tuberculosis. Towards the late 1800s, public health authorities in the United States and western Europe launched campaigns against public spitting and coughing, and the need for greater regulation of factory conditions, child labor, and poor housing.[97] These campaigns drew on a combination of workers, families, union activists, and public officials. According to Dyer, in 1904 the National Association for the Study and Prevention of Tuberculosis became the first nationwide voluntary health organization in the United States.[98] These types of organizations were followed by the introduction of anti-tuberculosis initiatives that ranged from anti-spitting campaigns between the public and private sector to fully fledged commissions across the world being established at the turn of the twentieth century.[99] The growth of these organizations provided the antecedents to the emergence of the International Union Against Tuberculosis and Lung Disease (hereafter the Union).

The period of 1888–1920 saw a process of conferences, campaigns, non-governmental and public activity signaling the need for an agency to coordinate the global response to tuberculosis. With the absence of a global public organization other than the League of Nation's failing Health Organization, the Union was established in 1920 as a confederation of associates that would develop consensus over a strategy to combat tuberculosis. The origins and role of the Union set an important precedent within global health governance, and resonate with the broader governance of health: where government will is lacking, particularly in the global context, forms of transnational social movements, with similar campaign strategies, for example, anti-spitting and the need for a cure for tuberculosis, emerge as an agenda-setter and implementer of global policies. A crucial factor in the founding of the union, however, were the advances in biomedicine taking place at the end of the 1800s.

Tuberculosis and chemotherapy

Efforts to combat both mycobacterium tuberculosis and mycobacterium bovis have been made possible by the findings of Robert Koch and Louis Pasteur. Koch developed Pasteur's work to prove the germ theory of tuberculosis contagion by identifying mycobacterium tuberculosis as the aerobic bacterium that causes tuberculosis, and crucially showing that the causes of bovine and human tuberculosis were not the same. Koch presented his findings on 24 March 1882 to much acclaim.[100] However, Koch had less success in translating his findings into an effective treatment for tuberculosis. His early development of tuberculin—a treatment made from the cultures of the tubercle bacilli organism—led to some improvements in patients' health in early trials but no long-term cure.[101] What Koch's discovery did was establish the foundations for further research into a vaccine. In 1906 Albert Calmette and Camille Guerin developed a vaccine—the Bacille-Calmette Guerin (BCG) vaccine—for the bovis strain of tuberculosis.[102] The vaccine was administered to a newborn human for the first time in 1921. The success of human trials led to France and countries under French influence administering the BCG, and exerting influence on the League of Nations Health Organization to certify its safety, as it did in 1928.[103] Presently, over 100 million infants are vaccinated with the BCG every year.[104]

For many the BCG does not make a significant impact on preventing tuberculosis and has failed to control adult pulmonary tuberculosis[105] but remains the only vaccine available. Part of the problem has been the ability of tuberculosis to adapt to the vaccine; the other problem has been to do with the governance of tuberculosis, and delays in implementing prevention methods such as the BCG and pasteurization.[106] As of 2003, the main objectives of vaccine research for tuberculosis have been to boost "the efficacy of neonatally administered BCG," to address the shortcomings of BCG, to address the issue of HIV and tuberculosis co-infection, and as with vaccines for malaria and HIV, to make any new vaccine affordable.[107] Any vaccination program, whether reliant on the BCG or introducing a new vaccine requires a mass campaign covering all children up to the age of five and an ongoing system in place for children born after the campaign.[108] Such campaigns require a high level of government coordination, local response, surveillance systems, and training of health workers. All of which are problematic in developing countries due to funds available, infrastructure, human resource capacity, and geographical scope.

Vaccination has been a significant tool in preventing the spread of tuberculosis, yet for some it was not until 1942 and the identification of the first "antibiotic" streptomycin by Selman Waksman that "the control of tuberculosis became a reality."[109] Waksman's identification of streptomycin resulted in him being awarded the Nobel Prize in Physiology or Medicine in 1952; however, it did not come without controversy. The streptomyces griseus organism that provided the basis of streptomycin was discovered not by Waksman, but by Albert Schatz and Elizabeth Bugie.[110] Moreover, it was thought by many that Jorgen

Lehman should have received greater recognition for his role in identifying para-amino salicylic acid (PAS), widely believed to be the first effective antibiotic to combat tuberculosis, and the basis for Waksman's discovery.[111] The controversy surrounding Waksman's discovery reflects the "celebrity" nature of scientists during this period of advancement, a range of men were singled out as pioneers of tuberculosis control and as such received a great deal of acclaim in the same way as new actors in global health governance outlined in Chapter 3.[112] The discovery of streptomycin gave way to the development of further means of chemotherapy treatment for tuberculosis such as isoniazid in 1952 and rifampin in 1966.[113] The purpose of chemotherapy to treat tuberculosis is to prevent death, the emergence of drug resistance, and transmission; however, to do so requires long-term treatment using a combination of drugs. Hence the use of rifampin or isoniazid alone is less successful.

Isoniazid and rifampin remain the first-line drugs for treatment of tuberculosis in most developing countries, despite the fact that strains of tuberculosis have become increasingly resistant. Multi-drug resistant (MDR) and extensively-resistant (XDR) tuberculosis has led to a call for improved treatment provision that is longer lasting but costly.[114] Effective treatment requires a combination of drugs, for example, for pregnant women the use of isoniazid and rifampin with pyrazinamide and ethambutol. Treating patients with HIV/AIDS and tuberculosis becomes more difficult with the need for different drug combinations and long-term treatment.[115] Treatment of MDR and XDR tuberculosis is problematic as it requires sufficient diagnosis and prescription of effective combination treatment, as well as the assumption that patients can pay for such treatment, or that they are able to take the treatment over a sustained period.[116] The cost often comes to bear on health workers, the local community or the individual patient.[117]

Part of the problem in providing such costly but effective treatment by public health interventions has been the decline in attention paid towards tuberculosis towards the end of the last century. Reichman argues that progress in combating tuberculosis in North America and Western Europe saw a decline in the amount of funding and priority afforded to the disease.[118] Tuberculosis became over-shadowed by other health concerns, specifically the emergence of HIV/AIDS. During this period the governance of tuberculosis in terms of agenda-setting, implementation, and provision was done by non-governmental actors as public interest began to wane. The Union in effect became "the operational arm" of the WHO's tuberculosis strategy.[119] The overarching recommendation of the WHO was for countries to adopt national strategies with a large level of support to community health

workers, health structures that are reflective of public demand, adequate training for all medical and non-medical staff, and the primacy
of the Ministry of Health in coordinating the national response.[120] At
the center of such recommendations was the need for community
involvement.[121] These two recommendations are reflective of wider
trends within global health governance during this period: institutional
inertia within the WHO and the repositioning of global health concerns from the global to the local as a means of keeping the cost down
and maximizing the voluntary nature of health provision. However,
without full-scale eradication or addressing the socio-economic drivers
of disease, or HIV, tuberculosis began to increase globally to the level
that could no longer be ignored.

DOTS and the Stop TB partnership

In 1993, the WHO declared tuberculosis a "global emergency."
Tuberculosis was on the increase in developing countries, it had a clear
impact on people living with HIV/AIDS, more people were becoming
resistant to treatment, and its prevalence was growing among the
poor, homeless, and migrant populations in industrialized countries
such as the United States.[122] These factors gave impetus for the all-
important political will needed to put tuberculosis at the top of the
global health agenda and to encourage the necessary funds to support
a clearly defined directive. The result of this was the introduction of
DOTS. DOTS was introduced by the WHO and partner organizations
such as the World Bank.[123] As its name would suggest, the primary
focus of DOTS was on effective treatment of the active disease to
control the global tuberculosis emergency by preventing an additional 12 million deaths from tuberculosis in 10 years. Drug treatment
had previously failed to address morbidity and mortality rates, specifically in developing countries, due to poor patient adherence and the
complicated nature of multi-drug resistance treatment, and the cost of
drug regimes.[124] DOTS rested on five principles: i) political and
administrative commitment; ii) case detection; iii) standardized short-
course chemotherapy treatment under direct observation; iv) effective
drug supply and management system; and v) monitoring, evaluation,
and accountability for every patient diagnosed.[125] The key measures
of success would be total number of cases detected and notified, and
successful adherence to treatment.[126] Beyond these core five principles, the DOTS approach also emphasized the need for new drugs,
vaccines, and advocacy strategies[127] to sustain the political relevance of
tuberculosis.

Similar to HIV/AIDS interventions, government involvement through national and local programs and the participation of all members of society were seen as integral to its successful implementation. The WHO established tuberculosis guidelines that emphasized the need for standardization of simple and applicable chemotherapy regimes; education for people and local communities affected by tuberculosis; government commitment and funding; and the importance of information systems and the supply of quality drugs.[128] In practical terms DOTS was focused at the local level, thus full participation and delivery capacity within local health centers and communities were essential components to full and effective implementation. Home support by family or community members would ensure adherence and patient encouragement.[129] All governments would adopt and implement these guidelines, and donors would pledge a minimum of 0.2 percent of their foreign aid budget to combating the disease.[130]

DOTS was a success in comparison to previous global tuberculosis programs. One hundred twenty-eight countries initially accepted the strategy, with 180 countries implementing the program by 2002, covering 69 percent of the world's population.[131] By 2005, the WHO reported that 26 million tuberculosis patients had been successfully treated between 1994 and 2005,[132] 90 percent of which had been from developing countries (Dyer 2010). Some countries saw a decline in tuberculosis prevalence, but in others tuberculosis control "remains a matter of conjecture."[133] The adoption and measurable output of DOTS established the strategy as a workable and successful model within and outside of the WHO. Ten years on, however, there was a need to continue to support DOTS interventions and expand its scope and relevance. Alongside this expansion plan was the strategy to manage the increasing problem of MDR tuberculosis, the DOTS-Plus Strategy.[134] DOTS-Plus would ensure the mandatory, rapid testing of MDR tuberculosis and a re-evaluation of surveillance strategies to target areas such as the Soviet Union that has been hesitant and in a degree of denial towards previous interventions.[135] DOTS was to be "more user-friendly"[136] for those using treatment and thus implemented in ways that community-based health services can cope with.[137] The result of this was the coming together of several initiatives at the turn of the millennium in support of tuberculosis interventions. These were: the Stop TB Partnership (1998–), the Global DOTS expansion plan (2001–5), and the inclusion of tuberculosis within Goal 5 of the MDGs.

Established in 1998, the Stop TB Partnership is a global alliance of NGOs organized to increase efforts to combat tuberculosis and intensify strategies and efforts.[138] The aim of the Stop TB Partnership is to align with the MDGs and DOTS Strategy to halve tuberculosis as a public health problem by 2015.[139] Stop TB focuses on the treatment and long-term elimination of the active disease. Similar to the role of the Union, Stop TB has established itself as a global authority and effective lobby group. As a partner organization, the WHO is able to use the alliance to secure support toward the successful realization of the DOTS strategy. In the same vein, the expertise and profile of the Stop TB Partnership allows it to make recommendations towards global policymaking that get the attention of decision-makers. This can be clearly seen by the development of ad hoc committee decisions, strategic plans, and contributions to WHO initiatives, such as the Global DOTS expansion plan.

The purpose of the Global DOTS expansion plan was to promote in-country coordination between different agencies, and the preparation of new national expansion plans to focus on individualized treatment.[140] The expansion of DOTS reasserted the role of governments and local communities in the coordination and implementation of tuberculosis strategies, specifically in reference to the growing problem of tuberculosis control in areas of high HIV prevalence.[141] National tuberculosis control programs would focus on a comprehensive approach to "high quality" expansion and enhancement of programs, health system strengthening, engaging care providers, and empowering local tuberculosis communities. As such, the WHO recommended the establishment of a central tuberculosis control unit within the ministry of health that would oversee the resources and technical support requirements of DOTS, ensure a sufficient standard of monitoring and evaluation, program management of the national policy, planning, and service networks, and social mobilization.[142] Service delivery would occur on a central–regional/province–district/peripheral level, similar to HIV/AIDS interventions being developed during this time. According to guidelines developed by the union in partnership with the WHO, the district level would be managed by a district coordinator who would ensure treatment adherence and enrolment, report results, and maintain supplies; the provincial level would similarly have a provincial/regional coordinator to supervise the districts, train personnel, coordinate with central officials and maintain quality of supply; and the central level would be run by a director of tuberculosis within the ministry of health to provide leadership and coordinate each of these functions.[143] This system shows parallels to the AIDS council system developed from 2000 onwards by the World Bank. However, the implementation of such a system was more ad hoc than that of the

AIDS councils, and in many ways, became fully operationalized at the same time as the AIDS councils. Through its association with HIV/AIDS, tuberculosis was able to receive further support and funding to fully establish those institutional structures in support of DOTS.

The mixed success of the DOTS strategy as the central mechanism to combat tuberculosis shows familiar patterns and lessons of global health governance. DOTS placed significant demands on the time of patients, local and national government, and community.[144] The emphasis on surveillance limited scope for flexibility and accommodation of the multiple demands on patients' time and the day-to-day difficulties not having access to money provides. For the strategy to be successful it required investment in equipment, supplies, and personnel.[145] Global politics continued to impact upon the realization of this health goal: economic crises and conflicts led to "erratic" supply of drugs, training of staff, and maintenance of health centers.[146] Those DOTS strategies that were successful were dependent on foreign aid, specifically World Bank loans.[147] This limited the sustainability of the project and the ability of governments to own and manage their interventions. The program often fell short of the US$10 million required annually to support it.[148] Screening was not popular in many states[149] but adopted as part of the wider recommendations of DOTS. Despite recommendations towards more effective governmental coordination, structures and units to combat tuberculosis were not as effectively established or decentralized until the introduction of HIV/AIDS funding and the association of national and district AIDS councils. Tuberculosis in many ways only became relevant and the DOTS fully operational and relevant after the resurgence of interest in HIV/AIDS. Finally, the tools needed to combat tuberculosis fully remained stuck in the innovations of the 1950s. Better vaccines and diagnostic materials, as well as the development and availability of better drugs for all still remain a problem.[150]

Resurgence and the future of tuberculosis

In 2002 Lee Reichman argued that MDR tuberculosis was a "time-bomb" in countries such as the Soviet Union.[151] The WHO suggested this strain of tuberculosis "was worrying."[152] During this time, DOTS had been operational for 10 years, and political will towards combating tuberculosis was on the increase, especially due to its association with HIV/AIDS. However, political will remained lacking in those all-important states with high prevalence rates and low expenditure on public health. This still remains the case. Despite calls for innovations for new strategies of tuberculosis treatment, prevention and eradication, issues of funding, disputes over biomedical research, and competing state interests make it a problem for global health governance. With the poverty gap widening, tuberculosis is set to continue as a contemporary problem for global health governance, and will continue to be declared a "global emergency" until the new tools, research developments, and sustained political and financial will exist to support treatment and eradication strategies. As with malaria new funding arrangements such as the Global Fund suggest some promise in sustained financing and investment in innovation to address both MDR and XDR tuberculosis. However, the longevity of such initiatives rests on how they stay relevant and elicit state and non-state support beyond their initial 10-year grace period, which as Chapter 3 highlighted, is increasingly in question.

Conclusion

The purpose of this chapter was to outline the practical and conceptual problems with governing the three biggest global health issues of the last 200 years: malaria, tuberculosis, and HIV/AIDS. Each of the diseases is different in their biology, longevity, and the mechanisms used to combat them, yet all show similarities in how they are governed, and the problems and opportunities therein. Each of the diseases has a sustained cause and effect relationship with poverty and development outcomes. This has led to debates and swings between vertical and horizontal, as well as biomedical and multisectoral, intervention strategies. A common theme across the three is to stress the importance of vaccination as a central mechanism of eradication, treatment, and prevention, despite its disproportionate cost to other simpler and more effective models of care, prevention, and treatment. Tools of prevention and treatment have had to evolve with the diseases as they mutate or replicate. This has required sustained funding of biomedical research, and the need to manage such research within wider governance mechanisms. Governance in this sense requires a combination of scientific, public health and policy expertise. For governance outcomes to be successful political will and financial support need to be continuous and sustained. Where state and intergovernmental interventions are not forthcoming, civil society and advocacy groups have played a pivotal role in highlighting the profile of these diseases and providing support for frontline services. Any gaps in funding reverse any progress made during periods of funding booms. This is a particularly pertinent lesson for the current HIV/AIDS response. The governance of these three diseases can thus be depicted by an over-arching emphasis on coordination, relevance, balance, and the continuous need to make the case for global responses based on secure and sustained funding. The three diseases compete for interest and resources in an ever-shrinking space. As the next chapter will show, without political interest and the funding that comes with it, health issues and strategies become neglected.

5   Neglected health

- Neglected tropical diseases (NTDs)
- Women as neglected health
- Health system strengthening as neglected health
- Conclusion

The dominance of issues such as HIV/AIDS and pandemic flu has for some led to the exclusion or neglect of other diseases and health priorities. Funding strategies that prioritize key health concerns ignore or skew the global health agenda away from common neglected tropical diseases that affect the most disadvantaged within society as well as broader health interventions such as the building of health centers and transportation routes. Neglected tropical diseases have become a category in their own right and have secured greater relevance and funding from private partnerships and foundations in recent years. However, narrowing neglect to specific diseases ignores the wide array of health concerns and strategies that one would assume to be at the core of global health governance. Thus the focus of this chapter is not only on neglected tropical diseases but neglected health more broadly. The chapter characterizes neglected health as those issues that are sidelined or ignored in favor of global prioritizing around specific issues, diseases, or agendas within global health governance. Two dominant areas of neglected health that are gaining wider attention have been health system strengthening and maternal health. Health system strengthening has been a core part of the governance of specific diseases but has been sidelined as a central strategy for good global health governance. Despite being included within the Millennium Development Goals (MDGs), up until 2010, maternal health has been ignored or bounded within categories of maternal-child-health-HIV. This chapter outlines how these issues have become neglected and the implications of neglecting, sidelining, and shifting between health issues for the long-term promotion of better health for all.

The chapter considers neglected health by first providing a general definition of neglected tropical disease before focusing on how these diseases have or have not been governed. The chapter explores the governance of maternal health: how it has been sidelined and why, what efforts are currently underway to combat maternal health, and what these efforts suggest about global health governance. The chapter then discusses the role of health system strengthening, how it can be framed as neglected health, and the implications of the vertical/ horizontal debate for global health interventions. The chapter concludes with a discussion as to what it means to be "neglected" and the utility in considering neglected health more broadly than neglected disease as a means of understanding global health governance.

Neglected tropical diseases (NTDs)

Neglected diseases are so defined because of the lack of political attention, intervention, or funding towards their prevention, treatment, or eradication. Seen as the "forgotten billion" neglected diseases are relatively easily treated and thus have greater possibility of eradication. The degree to which these diseases are neglected can vary but in the main the following diseases to fall under this category are: buruli ulcer, chagas diseases, cholera/diarrheal diseases, dengue, dracunculiasis (guinea-worm), endemic treponematoses, trypanosomiasis (sleeping sickness), leishmaniasis, leprosy, lymphatic filariasis, onchocerciais, schistosomiasis, soil-transmitted helminthiasis, and trachoma. These diseases tend to be located in poor, rural communities in developing countries with limited access to health provision. They arise from poor sanitation and nutrition, lack of access to safe drinking water, with conflict and natural disasters compounding these issues.

Despite the cost of treating and preventing such diseases being relatively cheap, few programs, funding initiatives, or state or non-state interventions exist to govern them. The reasons these diseases are neglected can be explained by the following tendencies within global health governance. First, health issues that become prioritized within global health governance have to be seen to carry a *global* threat. Neglected diseases tend to be localized in nature with minimal risk of spillover to the globe or urban populations in which international travelers are based. They tend to be non-infectious; those that are infectious are non-airborne and not transmitted through sexual contact. Hence they are no threat to the world population at large. Second, in being a local as opposed to a global threat, these diseases are not seen as a security concern. In general, they do not disproportionately affect armed forces, do not have the ability to destabilize a state, do not travel across borders, do not undermine the global economy, and cannot be used as a tool of bioterror. Thus they are less of a concern to those, richer, states that tend to finance global health initiatives. Third, the diseases lack incentive for investment. Whilst the need is large, the cost of treatment is low, requires minimal research and development investment, and thus less return for companies investing in the production of medicines to treat and prevent such illnesses. Medicines are cheap and easy to produce and thus do not entail any complex patent issues or high levels of return on a pharmaceutical company's investment. Finally, relatively little advocacy and media attention surrounds these diseases in comparison to other health issues. Neglected diseases in this regard lack the vogue funding element to them that is required to generate and sustain funding and political will. Neglected diseases suffer from problems common to many global health concerns: lack of effective treatment or access to treatment, better surveillance and diagnostic tools, the balance between vertical and inter-sectoral strategies, and the need to decrease the burden of disease. However, unlike other diseases and global health concerns, the political will to combat neglected tropical diseases is lacking.

The degree to which these diseases are neglected stems from the lack of state provision in their treatment and eradication, international aid financing towards them, and specialized agencies or partnerships established to address them in comparison to other diseases and health issues. They lack money, advocacy, political will or representation within global health. At the most institutional level, these diseases are represented within the World Health Organization (WHO) under the Tropical Disease unit through reports, initiatives, and partnerships for neglected disease. The WHO issues reports on various neglected diseases both individually and as a category, monitors specific epidemics, and highlights the problem of the "forgotten billion" in speeches made by the director-general. Key to the work of the unit is highlighting the results-based nature of investing in neglected disease to elicit wider funds. Such a results-based framework appeals to the paradigm of global health interventions developed by the new institutions outlined in Chapter 3.

The WHO has renewed its emphasis upon neglected diseases, with its 2008–15 Global Plan to Combat Neglected Disease highlighting both the WHO's role and track record for effectiveness in these areas. Similar to the WHO's general approach to combating health concerns, the plan highlights a horizontal approach to the issue, stressing the role of population-based as opposed to disease-specific interventions. These interventions are to be based on a multi-disease, "intersectoral" approach that focuses on neglected diseases and health systems as a single category when identifying prevention and treatment strategies[1] as opposed to focusing on specific disease eradication or elimination. The rationale for such an approach is that populations are not vulnerable to a single neglected tropical disease and that prevention and treatment strategies for some neglected diseases are also relevant to others. Hence, any approach must address multiple tropical diseases as well as strengthening the overarching health systems that support them. Strengthening health systems in this regard refers to the capacity of health staff in-country, particularly in rural clinics, and the development and deployment of improved tools for prevention and diagnostics, and high-quality medicines.[2] Innovation is key to this, but a central part of the WHO's work has been to advocate for greater access to such innovation. The implementation of the Global Plan would be justified through World Health Assembly (WHA) resolutions and the regions.

Common to the problems with funding outlined in Chapters 2 and 3, the WHO is constricted in the amount of effort and material resources it has to address neglected diseases. On the one hand, they present a low-cost initiative that could produce results for the beleaguered institution, yet on the other hand they lack the political interest or concern of member states that fund it. Moreover, as an institution that prioritizes its in-state partnerships and collaborations and is based on a decentralized model, the WHO is less able to implement widespread grand country-specific projects on neglected disease. Hence much of its activity rests on partnerships. The WHO identifies itself as having "pioneered" partnerships to provide better access to treatment and surveillance systems[3] through collaborations with the Global Alliance to Eliminate Lymphatic Filiariasis, Global Buruli Ulcer Initiative, Partners for Parasite Control and Global Collaboration for Development of Pesticides for Public Health. Perhaps one of the most significant partnerships between the WHO and private actors has been that with the Bill and Melinda Gates Foundation.

As Chapter 2 highlighted, the Bill and Melinda Gates Foundation has become a key player within global health governance. One of the overarching priorities of their global health program has been neglected tropical disease. The Gates Foundation's strategy for neglected disease prioritizes the key areas of control, elimination, and eradication through: vaccine development, early detection through improved diagnostics, control of the source, elimination of diseases to undetectable levels, and full eradication of specific diseases. The foundation's main focus towards eradication has concentrated on Guinea Worm disease. Working in partnership with the Carter Centre, the foundation has contributed to a decline in Guinea Worm to almost total eradication, with only 5,000 cases in total reported in Sudan, Ghana, Ethiopia and Mali in 2010. In partnership with the WHO, the Centers for Disease Control and Prevention (CDC), United Nations Children's Fund (UNICEF), and United States Agency for International Development (USAID), the foundation has concentrated its elimination efforts on neglected diseases such as sleeping sickness and onchocerciasis. Neglected tropical diseases appeal to the foundation because of their ability to provide safe return on investment, not in terms of profit but effective results and in some cases, potential eradication. Disease eradication and results regardless of the global impact of the disease can perform a key legitimating function for the foundation and its wider role in global health governance. According to Strassburg, eradication of disease depends on the following key components: the natural history of disease; the appropriate control measures available; mortality; morbidity; cost benefits; time period; and funding availability.[4] With neglected disease the first of these six factors have been clear, with the last being the most problematic. However, Gates Foundation involvement in neglected tropical diseases suggests this is changing.

The global resurgence of interest in neglected tropical disease by multilateral institutions such as the WHO and World Bank, private actors such as the Gates Foundation, and bilateral investment from USAID, specifically the CDC, suggests eradication may be possible. Eradication, however, will only become possible when financial investment towards neglected disease matches the rhetoric of alliances and networks created to address this global health challenge. As Figure 5.1 shows, investment in neglected tropical diseases peaked in 2007, with large-scale investment from partnerships such as the Global Alliance for Vaccines and Immunisation (GAVI), and the less recognized Belgian government.

In 2009, the Gates Foundation widely perceived to be a principle investor in neglected disease, only spent US$120,970. In comparison the total budget to combat HIV/AIDS amounted to US$221,648. The Foundation's commitment shown in Figure 5.1 can mainly be seen through the investments it made to the GAVI during this time. What Figure 5.1 does suggest is that despite the emergence of the partnership decade for global health, it is bilateral donors and the World Bank that have sustained investment in neglected disease, with new initiatives leading to year-specific funding peaks. Despite the rhetoric of further initiatives for neglected tropical diseases, consistency in funding continues to be provided by "old" institutions of global health governance, particularly the World Bank.

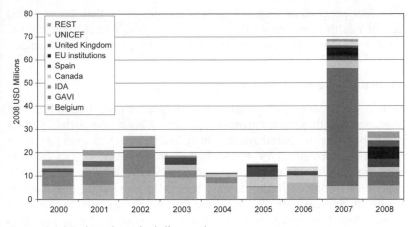

Figure 5.1 Neglected tropical disease donors

The World Bank has had a consistent role in funding neglected tropical disease initiatives since the 1970s. The 1974 Onchocerciasis Control Program was the first disease and health-specific program launched by the World Bank[5] in partnership with the WHO, Food and Agriculture Organization (FAO), and United Nations Development Programme (UNDP). The targeting of health concerns, specifically neglected tropical diseases was a central component of Robert McNamara's presidency of the bank. McNamara proposed the initiative in 1973 in a memorandum to the board of the executive directors.[6] The World Bank's approach to onchocerciasis and other neglected diseases follows a similar model to its overarching approach to global health. All programs highlight the role of governments and country ownership, and reflect the need for multi-sectoral interventions that include non-health-specific implementers. This approach has been disease-specific vertical interventions based on sustained investment. However, as part of the bank's wider shift towards health system strengthening, investment in neglected tropical diseases has become increasingly more integrated into broader health programs.

As efforts to combat HIV/AIDS, tuberculosis and malaria have proven increasingly difficult, neglected diseases have come to the wider attention of institutions of global health and those that finance them. Neglected diseases have benefited from the introduction of new actors in global health and a growing network of advocacy surrounding particular neglected diseases such as cholera and sleeping sickness, meaning that they occupy one category less, and are not so neglected. The growth of attention towards neglected diseases can also be seen as part of a wider program of vertical health interventions, so that the neglected area of health is no longer this group of tropical diseases but are the broader categories of health system strengthening, women, and gender.

Women as neglected health

Women and gender are a space of neglected health. The WHO and associated health agencies promote gender equity within a rights-based framework, yet the paradigm in which health policy is made exists in either a gender-neutral or gender-biased frame. Pertinent to this has been the growth of interest in maternal and child health, and the inclusion of women's health as only being that in relation to childcare, childbirth, and caring roles within the family; and minimal application of how health interventions affect men and women differently. This section outlines how women have been included in global health policy, by first concentrating on the WHO's Gender, Women and Health Network. The section will then consider the previous sidelining and then growing recognition of efforts to improve maternal and child health, and the role such efforts have in perpetuating gender stereotypes that limit a broad gender-based approach to women's health. The section will then draw together what gender, women, maternal, and child health mean for neglect in global health governance.

Women and gender strategies

The WHO's Gender, Women and Health Network provides the over-arching framework for the inclusion of women and gender difference within global health governance. The network emphasizes gender-based approaches to health governance that recognize how various diseases and health issues affect women differently. In addition, the Network places a particular emphasis on the interdependent relationship between gender equality and health in the realization of MDGs 3, 4, 5, and 6.[7] The main areas of focus for the network are issues of gender and HIV/AIDS, malaria and climate change, gender-based violence, and gender mainstreaming across the WHO's activities. The Network pursues these objectives through: i) capacity-building for gender analysis and action; ii) mainstreaming gender within the WHO's management; iii) promotion of disaggregated data based on sex and gendered analysis; and iv) accountability for gender mainstreaming activities within the WHO.[8] These activities are mainstreamed throughout the organization and in partnership with states though Geneva headquarters and representation in each of the six regional offices.

International health agencies recognize the role and importance of women's health in the promotion of better health outcomes for all. The United Nations Population Fund (UNFPA) sees women's health as beyond the narrow confines of maternal and child health to include gender-based violence, female genital mutilation, women in emergency situations, and the role of women in health delivery as carers for others. In so doing, the agency highlights how women's needs must be met to support their own development as well as that of others.[9] The World Bank similarly highlights the role of women's health as fundamental to wider development processes, but moreover highlights how women are an untapped source of potential for growth and development in low-income economies. For the bank, healthier mothers are central to investing in the well-being of children and their future productivity as adults, as such "investments in reproductive health have multiple payoffs for families, communities, and the national economy."[10] Hence women's health in this respect is understood in relation to economic development.

The efficacy of these activities, however, remains questionable. The WHO Network promotes gender equality through annual reports, advocacy on International Women's Day, discussion forums, and emphasizing best practice. However, these issues are often sidelined for more gender-neutral or specific health policies or programs. The World Bank is meant to mainstream gender approaches to health across its projects and programs, yet in effect this is dependent on the project, or more specifically the interest of the project leader. Similar to the WHO, the bank has a Gender and Development Unit that engages in the same sort of activities as the gender network, yet in the main gender difference, how women experience health differently goes ignored. Gender mainstreaming to promote the inclusion of women in policy takes priority over a gendered lens of how not only health issues affect men and women differently but how interventions and projects affect women and men differently. The only progress that has been made in recognizing gender and women in global health governance has been that of their role in Goals 4 and 5 of the MDGs: maternal and child health.

Maternal and child health: responding to neglect

Women's health has increasingly become conflated with MDGs 4 and 5. MDG 4 seeks to reduce child mortality under 5 by two-thirds between 1990 and 2015, and increase child immunization against measles. MDG 5 has the overarching aim of decreasing the maternal mortality ratio by two-thirds between 1990 and 2015 through increased access to contraception and antenatal care, and the training of health professionals, specifically midwives. The purpose of this goal is to address the 350,000 birth-related deaths per year, 99 percent of which take place in developing countries. Goal 4 has been met with initial success in the early stages of efforts to achieve the MDGs. By 2008, child deaths under five had declined from 100 to 72 per 1,000 births 1990–2008, vaccine research and distribution were prioritized by actors such as UNICEF, and widespread immunization initiatives were supported by donors and states.[11] However, further progress towards the implementation of these goals has been halted by continued problems with nutritional provision, health infrastructure and support systems, and a wider association with and importance attributed to child health.

Up until 2009, Goal 5 was an arena of neglected health. Initial efforts towards the health MDGs concentrated on AIDS, tuberculosis, and malaria, skewing the agenda towards prevention of mother-to-child HIV transmission only, and showed less concern for broader strategies to invest in tools of maternal health provision such as training midwives, education, nutritional support, and greater access to health centers. Half of all spending towards population-based initiatives (in which maternal health is often categorized) during 1999–2009 was spent on HIV/AIDS.[12] Since 2009, this neglect has been recognized and as such there has been a reassertion of effort through the Global Strategy for Women's and Children's Health (2010); UNFPA's Safe Motherhood Strategy; and the Global Consensus on Maternal and Neonatal Health (2009). The Global Consensus is a commitment of 41 bilateral and multilateral development agencies in support of: i) leadership and engagement; ii) evidence-based interventions through quality care and health systems; iii) free services for women and children at the point of use "if countries choose to provide them"; iv) skilled health workers; and v) monitoring, evaluation, and accountability.[13] The Global Strategy for Women's and Children's Health provides the over-arching framework in which these initiatives and further interventions into MDGs 4 and 5 operate.

The central premise of the strategy is to support and develop country strategies for maternal health, integrate health service delivery, and strengthen health systems and workforce through innovative approaches to health financing and improved monitoring and evaluation.[14] The role of development partners within this is to coordinate the response and generate wider funds in support through ensuring donor countries fulfill their commitments to the Paris Declaration and Monterrey Consensus in facilitating private–public partnerships. The strategy outlines key targets and roles and responsibilities for governments, donors, multilateral organizations, civil society, the business community, healthcare workers, and academic and research institutions, all emphasizing the need for coordination, innovation, training of healthcare workers, and sustained support for the issue.[15]

Leading these interventions has been the Health 4+ (UNFPA, UNICEF, the World Bank and the WHO) with individual and joint strategic plans aimed at combating this problem. The purpose of the Health 4+ is to highlight the problem of maternal and child health within the MDGs by working with states and civil society in mainstreaming these issues within state-based agendas and health planning, scaling up health services through resource provision and technical support, monitoring and evaluation, and the provision of long-term projects that address the root causes of maternal mortality and morbidity. Key to this is the gendered dimensions of the problem. Each of these actors adopts the Global Strategy for Women's and Children's Health to align with their own objectives and interventions. The WHO has the overarching responsibility for coordinating the strategy. In support of the strategy and as a wider acknowledgment of the organization's commitment, the Department of Maternal, Newborn, Child and Adolescent Health is to be launched in 2011.[16] The purpose of the Department is to implement the WHO's vision of universal coverage, sustained interventions, collaboration between multiple partners, commitment of members of government, and overall a greater value placed on pregnancy, childbirth, post-partum, and newborn care. It supports this vision through advocacy, partnership, monitoring and evaluation, and technical country support, as well as resource mobilization and capacity-building.

UNFPA have had a fundamental role in maternal and child health, being a lead agency before and in the formation of the MDGs. The 1994 International Conference on Population and Development, Cairo established the foundations for MDGs 4 and 5 to build on. The Cairo conference explicitly linked stabilizing population growth with poverty eradication and development, and the need to provide resources to help stabilize population in such a way as to promote the notion that every child is wanted, all births safe, people to be HIV-free, and women and girls to be treated with dignity and respect.[17] This approach has framed wider interventions into reproductive health, and provides the outline for organizations such as the African Union's activities in the field. The UNFPA has developed the principles of the Cairo conference in line with the MDGs to promote "Safe Motherhood" through provision of women's access to contraception and skilled care at birth, and access to timely and quality emergency care.[18] This strategy is promoted in partnership with states and donor partners to the UNFPA, as well as the establishment of the 2008 Maternal Health Thematic Fund. As a complement to the UNFPA's framework, UNICEF conducts an advocacy role in promoting the importance of maternal health and the need for more healthcare workers in developing countries, and demonstrating awareness of the issues across its wider programs.[19]

The World Bank has interpreted the Global Strategy for Women's and Children's Health through its 2010–15 action plan, *Better Health for Women and Families*. This plan highlights the neglect of MDG 5, and has the overarching aim of injecting financial and advocacy support to the following areas similar to the UNFPA: contraception, skilled attendance at birth, health worker training, education of girls, knowledge and prevention transferral, and close alignment with health agencies.[20] Underpinning this approach is the Bank's renewed focus on health system strengthening since the late 2000s that stresses the role of infrastructure, skills and referral pathways as the main issues pertaining to working and appropriate Maternal and Reproductive Health Services. The Bank's maternal health interventions follow the same framework developed in its HIV/AIDS interventions discussed in Chapter 4. The Action Plan prioritizes support for state infrastructure and decentralizing financial flows to the poorest in society through initiatives such as cash transfers and partnerships with civil society organizations, nominally community groups.[21]

Perhaps one of the most obvious omissions from the Health 4+ has been the United Nations Development Fund for Women (UNIFEM), now UN Women. UNIFEM as it existed up to 2011 did not have a prominent role in the realization of the health MDGs, or women's health more broadly, despite being the main UN institution for women. UNIFEM did not have a direct role within WHO planning for MDGs 4 and 5, is often sidelined from decision-making by being represented by UNDP more broadly, and only has advisory or watchdog capacity with little funds or mandate to implement policy through programs and projects on the ground. UNIFEM did not have a direct budget allocation for funding programs or projects in MDGs 4 and 5, but instead developed knowledge and advocacy to raise awareness of women's issues and the MDGs. It did so through training, technical support, encouraging women's participation in leadership and decision-making, and highlighting discrimination. UNIFEM contributed to the realization of the MDGs by strengthening female capacity in all of the UN's operations and using sex-disaggregated data to evaluate progress and any gender gaps in provision.[22] The role of UNIFEM was important in this regard as it highlights how gender-based institution and the broader issue of gender are on the whole sidelined from interventions into maternal and child health, and women's health more broadly. Women's health has thus far not been identified as a focal point of UN Women beyond the MDGs. It is too early to know the role the new agency will have within global health, but should it follow the path of UNIFEM this role will be minimal.

Women's health as maternal-child-health

The increased interest in maternal health in particular, suggests that women's health is far from neglected. However, this assumes that women's health is narrowly understood as only relating to their role as mother or carer. How women experience health services and different illnesses and concerns is not considered within wider processes of global health governance. Women's health is a concern only in relation to gender-specific roles. This re-enforces their position as implementers and workers within global health governance that carry out projects at the local level. Women are positioned within global health as tools of ensuring the health and thus future development of broader populations, with their needs, health concerns, and experiences coming second. International institutions and agencies recognize this is a problem; however, such recognition is often sidelined in favor of positioning women with the burden of providing better health outcomes for their families. For example, the World Bank's Action Plan for Maternal Health only includes an acknowledgment to the separation of women's health from maternal health in the appendices of the report, with little mention within the main body.

The lack of a gendered approach or lens to how women experience health and health interventions differently is clear when considering the content and homogeneity of Strategic Plans and Action Plans for maternal and child health. In many cases, these strategies follow similar frameworks to those developed in response to the global HIV/ AIDS epidemic, highlighting the need for participation, country ownership, community involvement, and innovation. The only difference is the emphasis placed on health system strengthening and incentivizing wider training of midwives and health specialists. This inclusion is less about specific health interventions, however, but has more to do with the renewed interest in the all important but often neglected area of health system strengthening. In conflating women's health with maternal and child health and adopting homogenous programs that are similar to existing vertical health interventions, women and gender difference becomes hidden from the policy process and women's role within global health governance continues to be that of mother-or-carer of the new generation. Women's needs, experiences, and difference thus become neglected within the policy and decision-making aspect of global health.

Health system strengthening as neglected health

The debate between vertical disease-specific and horizontal systems-based health interventions has typified problems of how to govern health and divided the institutions that do. Despite a keen assertion from actors in global health that such a division does not exist, problems of basic healthcare provision in line with the objectives and outlook developed within the Alma Ata Declaration remain. The WHO has been the central proponent of the need for health system strengthening; much of the decline in attention towards health systems reflects that of the salience and relevance of the WHO to global health governance. This section positions arguments for and against the idea that health systems are a form of neglected health.

The central issue that highlights a decline or neglect towards health system strengthening has been the disproportionate amount of funds earmarked for HIV/AIDS, tuberculosis, and malaria. The advocacy and support channeled towards the three diseases in combination with vertical strategies towards neglected disease eradication has seen a shift of funding away from health system needs such as transport and infrastructure, procurement, local health centers, and staff capacity by donor states and the public. Old institutions such as the World Bank and new institutions such as the Global Fund have prioritized vertical interventions into healthcare. The associated financing they offer eclipses that of the WHO and hence the activities within developing countries become that of vertical interventions that ignore health system strengthening because international funds are not available to support it. Hence health system strengthening becomes neglected within the public domain.

Perhaps the biggest indication of neglect towards health system strengthening in recent years has been its omission from the MDGs, that as Chapter 3 demonstrated have focused on specific health goals rather than the more complex structural or systemic issues underpinning ill-health. Goal 5 specifically galvanized the G8 into establishing the Global Fund as well as a range of bilateral and multilateral initiatives. The three "health goals" constructed the global priorities for health and development; hence isolating other pertinent factors to their realization such as health system strengthening and social and economic inequalities. The health goals by their very nature are narrow in focus as a means of simplifying the problem of development to make efforts to combat poverty more straightforward to the populations and states that support anti-poverty initiatives. The remit of these goals, hence, does not extend to issues relating to the structural determinants of poverty and ill-health and more thorny issues such as the "brain drain" of health professionals from less developed to developed countries.

The "brain drain" element of health professionals leaving less developed countries to work abroad points to a further explanation as to why health system strengthening is neglected. At the core of providing the essentials of better health systems—access to affordable medicines, procurement, distribution, the development and staffing of health centers—is the need to address some of the challenges of economic globalization. These challenges include issues of labor rights, intellectual property, and global inequalities that distort the pay scales of health professionals in different states. Globalization has made governing health difficult, not only in terms of the spread of infectious disease and the number of actors involved in governance, but the multiplicity and overlap of concerns, and the embedded nature of problems within the global political economy. Governing global health has come to be about framing complex but specific global health problems in such a way that they have measurable targets and clear outcomes for investment of both money and public interest without tackling the basic needs or root causes of ill-health.

The shift towards results-oriented approaches to funding for global health has the following implications for wider recognition of health system strengthening. First, health system strengthening needs to identify key priorities and issues that can be measured as proven deliverables in return for health system financing. Donors, institutions, and states should be able to track funds and measure success. Second, factors associated with health system strengthening, for example, travel networks, road building and procurement, need to be framed in such a way that clearly stipulates the health benefits of investment. The structural nature of problems with health system strengthening makes it difficult to isolate the relevance of specific issues such as transportation to better, and crucially measurable, outcomes. Third, advocates of health system strengthening will have to incorporate multisectoral interventions, to address some of the structural limitations to successful implementation, for example, highways agencies for road-building, local planning offices for health centers, and education systems to support staff capacity-building. Fourth, health system strengthening will have to be mainstreamed across multiple health interventions, as a core element of any results-based framework to highlight its relevance and attract wider funds. Finally, this has implications for the WHO in how it positions its operations within wider approaches to results-based initiatives, and how they are defined in terms of global health. For results-based frameworks to be effective in health system strengthening, the WHO in partnership with states from both developed and developing countries needs to identify what constitutes a measure of success, and how to account for those factors that cannot be measured. How measurement and success are framed is central to the future of global health governance, what becomes prioritized, and what becomes neglected. Should these factors go unaddressed, health system strengthening will continue to be neglected in comparison to other vertical interventions.

The notion that health system strengthening is a form of neglected health is a controversial assertion. It remains the primary focus of the WHO's activities, part of the institution's core mandate and thus underpins all activities in global health. Institutions, partnerships, and donors involved in more vertical, disease, or country-specific strategies all reiterate their wider role in health system strengthening. Despite the predominance of vertical interventions into key diseases dominating the shift from international to global health, health system strengthening has become increasingly recognized as central to the operations of disease-specific projects and institutions. The main explanation for this is that on a practical level vertical interventions rely on effective running health systems. Health systems are essential for the procurement and distribution of drugs, prevention strategies, and the development of health centers to distribute and monitor HIV, malaria, and tuberculosis. The result of this is many organizations and projects that have been vertically conceived, engage in forms of health system strengthening as a means of supporting wider projects. At the same time programs that center on health systems have framed their activities and plans in such a way that ally with the big three diseases as a means of securing wider funding support. Hence, where a program or project does not explicitly address health systems, most programs engaged with implementation of health programs implicitly do. In this sense the neglect of health system strengthening does not relate to the practice of engaging in such activities, but relates to the framing of funding priorities in such a way that directly highlights system strengthening as a key priority of global health.

The inclusion, or lack thereof, of health system strengthening within global health financing and project development is changing. The

World Bank has highlighted health system strengthening as one of the three main priorities of the Health, Nutrition and Population unit's activities and a key barrier to the effective realization of the MDGs. The Global Fund, established to engage in vertical interventions continues to discuss health system strengthening both at the board and secretariat level, and whilst not highlighting it as a funding priority, has been keen to demonstrate the impact its grant portfolio has on health systems. The Bill and Melinda Gates Foundation is keen to assert that health system strengthening is a fundamental part of its grantee activities. A similar thread throughout these organizations is that the debate between horizontal and vertical interventions is a tired one and that by their very nature all organizations and funding bodies are working towards the same aim and thus partake in multiple activities. Whilst specific programs have not necessarily highlighted the health system strengthening aspect of their operations, this has often been taken as a given. What the debate around vertical and horizontal approaches to global health has done is to put health systems strengthening back in the spotlight, for organizations, states, and donors to be much more explicit as to how they are undertaking programs to strengthen health systems. This has two implications for this debate: i) health system programs continue to be neglected as stand-alone projects, but are just integrated into existing vertical interventions; or ii) the health system is not and has never been neglected in practice, programs towards health system strengthening have just been implicitly applied.

Conclusion

The financially driven nature of global health governance necessitates neglect of certain health issues or diseases at any one time. Neglect is a constant fear and threat for advocates of specific health issues, as specialists compete in a narrow terrain to express their relevance and success rates so as to maintain support. As Chapter 4 demonstrated, shifts away from vertical interventions can lead to the resurgence of major pandemics, yet investment in specific issues is hard to sustain. However, issues such as health system strengthening and women's health are a fundamental part of global health governance: to promote health for all, rights-based approaches, and the ability of individuals to look after their own health in exchange for basic services from the state. Yet, these issues are also susceptible to the vagaries of global financing for health. Global health governance thus comes to be about a balance between sustaining core features for provision: equity for men and women through the recognition of difference and the provision of accessible, equipped, and adaptable health systems that are fully staffed and responsive to the needs of individuals. If the infrastructure part of global health continues to be sidelined, individuals will further lack the incentive to maintain their health needs and concerns. It is important thus to consider neglect more broadly in terms of health than just disease.

6 Conclusion

- **What is global health governance?**
- **Multiple and competing actors**
- **Partnerships and the public–private divide**
- **Individual rights and scientific progress**
- **Global health governance for whom?**

Global health governance resembles a complex interplay of multiple public and private actors with competing approaches to how health for all can or should be realized, and differing ideas as to which health issues should be prioritized. The purpose of this book has been to untangle this interplay, to outline the main conceptual approaches to governing global health, the institutions that do so, and why certain health issues receive lots of attention to the detriment of other concerns, and, crucially, why this matters. This chapter draws together the main findings of the book to provide a conclusion as to what global health governance is. It does so by focusing on the balancing act between different actors, the public and the private, individual rights and progress, before reflecting on who or what global health governance is for.

What is global health governance?

Global health governance is about the management of multiple transboundary health concerns among competing interests, resources, and time periods. The globalized nature of health concerns and threats have necessitated coordinated action among states, civil society organizations, the private sector, and intergovernmental organizations in tackling these issues. Emerging from the nineteenth century with the growth of global trade and the golden age of discovery, health governance was principally interested in infectious, air, and water-borne diseases that did not discriminate among populations. Since this time, global health governance has had to develop to respond to new threats such as avian flu and HIV/AIDS as well as the recurring presence of old problems such as tuberculosis. New institutions, processes, and partnerships have formed to address such concerns. These structures and processes in turn have developed to address much more than infectious diseases, to concentrate on lifestyle and behavior choice, chronic illnesses, the need for standardization, and most importantly the socio-economic and political drivers of ill-health in the world.

As health threats have become globalized so have the drivers of ill-health and how states respond to them. It is efforts to address the drivers of poor health that has made global health governance a much more political than technocratic enterprise. Good global health is intrinsic to economic growth through trade and the expansion of financial services to developing countries. Good health within a population increases labor productivity and boosts individual esteem and confidence in the political system. Hence, good health where people are able to live productive lives is an intrinsic component to any form of social or economic development and an end to world poverty. Health—whether susceptibility to disease, poor living conditions, or access to food and clean water—is the key indicator of absolute global poverty and inequality. The wealth, modernity, or success of a country can be assessed not only by the health of the economy, but the health of the population. Global health governance matters because it is pertinent to the successful realization of an end to poverty, international development, and peace and security.

For global health governance to be effective it requires cooperation from individuals, families, businesses, civil society, the state, the market, and intergovernmental organizations. In·this sense, global health governance can be best understood as a balancing act between different dichotomies: multiple actors involved in decentralized implementation and globally centralized decision-making; the public and private sector; and maintaining the rights of individuals and sovereign states whilst delivering and promoting advancements in scientific discovery and knowledge.

Multiple and competing actors

For most, global health governance is characterized by the World Health Organization (WHO). Established in 1948 from the antecedents of nineteenth-century arrangements for global health protection, at the core of the organization is the need to respond to existing and emerging health threats and to address the socio-economic causes of poor health within a rights-based framework. The WHO is the lead intergovernmental organization for global health and sets the framework in which multiple institutions work. However, while its legitimacy is in no doubt, its authority, influence and reliability have been questioned by internal problems and an increasingly competitive terrain of actors and interests. For many, the WHO lacks the ability to fully address the socio-economic drivers of poor health which has opened the field to financial development agencies such as the World Bank and bilateral donors to set the global agenda, specifically in regard to certain diseases. The WHO has been unable to fully compete with or harness the private financing of scientific and technological research and innovation, or balance such financing with wider issues of access and equity in distribution of any scientific advancement. Moreover, as Chapter 2 suggests, the WHO has been subject to internal wrangling as to its mandate and emphasis on specific diseases and health issues at the cost of a wider agenda towards health system strengthening. Combined, these factors have led to an opening of space for multiple actors to engage with health concerns. As this book has shown, global health governance is not only about the WHO but multiple state-based, public, private bodies, civil society organizations, individuals and partnerships that come together to respond to specific issues or the promotion of good health more broadly.

The presence of multiple actors has mixed outcomes. On the one hand, it has shown a positive increase in investment of all total development assistance for health, and a genuine partnership and commitment of multisectoral actors from different backgrounds with various interests. This has allowed for specialism and representation of all aspects of global society. It makes the management of global health much more diffuse. On the other hand, it complicates how global health is managed as responsibility and accountability become hard to track as it is unclear as to who is doing what, how, and to what outcome. Moreover, such multisectorality tends to be defined by who has the most financial clout or positional influence. Such influence can skew the agenda, prioritize specific issues, and make global health governance less about health and health systems but more about specific diseases. In practice, the varying degrees of influence within global health mean that although multiple actors are involved in implementation, decision-making and agenda-setting is hierarchical and set within global cities where key institutions and actors are clustered, for example, Geneva, Washington, DC, and New York. Hence, global health governance is a balance between diffusion of implementation and involvement with a globally hierarchical and centered arena of decision-making.

A centralized system of global health governance promotes a degree of homogeneity in how health issues are responded to as it crowds out alternative agendas for action, and uses a results-based system where if one policy is seen to work it is applied to multiple health contexts. The application of one successful model to multiple health issues obscures space for recognizing different health issues that require specific responses. Planning and agenda-setting within global health governance tend to occur through the drawing up of global strategy plans at the international level, say in the WHO in Geneva or the World Bank in Washington, DC, that are then tailored to regional or national contexts with little recognition of cultural, political, or gender difference. Global health governance is increasingly decentralized in terms of practice, but the main agenda-setting remains global.

Partnerships and the public–private divide

Wider inclusion within processes of decision-making in global health governance has occurred through a balance between the public and private sector and institutionalized forms of partnership. Public and private actors share a common interest in the promotion of good health for the well-being of the world's population. However, the motivation and reward involved with this common interest can differ from the well-being of a population being a good in itself and profit as a means of reinvesting in health. Global health has always been linked to trade flows, intellectual property, and investment from the private sector. In this sense, outcomes for better global health have always depended on fluctuations in the market in terms of money available for public investment in health, and incentives for investment in specific research and development of new technologies. However, as the 1980s and early 1990s have shown, an increase in market-oriented approaches to health can also distort investment in health services and sideline rights-based approaches to health. The introduction of market-oriented policies in developing countries during the 1980s led to under-investment in health by states constricted by economic reform or a domestic private sector that had yet to flourish. Whilst the inclusion of market-oriented approaches to global health governance should produce results-based initiatives that are shown to be cost-effective, efficient, and expertised, these interventions need to be balanced against wider forms of social protection and sustainability on the part of the state. Where the state is cumbersome and bureaucratic, the private sector has a clear role. The potential for both the public sector to safeguard the interests and rights of individuals, and the private sector to fill the gaps in public provision and introduce new ideas has been balanced through the rise of partnerships.

The balance between private and public interventions in global health has become institutionalized within global health governance through the types of new partnerships discussed in Chapter 4. The rise of partnerships and multiple arrangements for the production of better health outcomes can be seen as positive. These partnerships have overcome the either/or argument between public and private investment by combining the strengths of both. Partnerships show a commitment to promote health for all and widespread recognition that global health is at the cornerstone of an end to poverty, economic growth, peace, and political stability. In addition it suggests a balance between the market and non-market interventions can be recognized, institutionalized, and applied to practice. This commitment and coordination suggests that an international regime of shared norms and values has emerged to support global health efforts. Global health in this sense is made up of multiple issue-specific regimes that overlap and coordinate to fulfill a wider function. At the heart of this are the norms of: a rights-based approach to health, equality and liberty of the individual, and the need for a mixture of public–private intervention.

However, to see global health governance simply as a regime depoliticizes some of the processes and wrangling between actors. Whilst a specific language of global health based on acronyms and innovative ideas has permeated many actors, projects and discussions within global health governance, beyond the need to improve people's health and welfare, no norm as to how this should be achieved has been agreed upon. Global health governance thus presents the idea of a regime for common action and agreement, but this regime tends to be hierarchical, and characterized by confusion and in some cases dissent among different actors surrounding specific issues of contention, for example how to effectively prevent the spread of HIV transmission. The regime built around global health governance differs from comparable regimes such as the environment in that it is well funded, appears collaborative between scientific communities, the public and private sector, and possesses a common political will towards the promotion of health as a public good. However, it is political will that makes some of these partnerships fractious or contentious, as scientific knowledge and expertise or technological innovation is set against individual freedom or choice.

Individual rights and scientific progress

Political will to promote better health outcomes exists within global health governance in regards to global initiatives, sustained funding support for health issues during 2000–10, and declarations of intent. However, all actors in global health governance lack some form of political will—that is, the will or interest to promote better health outcomes. For example, a state may lack the will or ability to provide infrastructure to support the widespread distribution of insecticide-treated bed nets for malaria; an individual may lack the will to stop eating fatty and sugary foods despite the threat of diabetes and other obesity-related chronic health concerns; a church may lack the will to provide condoms for people living with HIV; a local community may choose to stigmatize people living with elephantitis. Each of these scenarios relates to issues of knowledge, faith, money, and esteem, or a lack of will to engage in broader global strategies. Hence, processes of global health governance come to constitute the construction of will to act in a certain way. Global health governance is about constructing will to act or change based on a specific form of knowledge that balances scientific research and expertise against the beliefs, knowledge, and liberty of individuals and society. The problem of constructing the will to act, whether it be for a state to invest in health systems or individuals to engage in behavior that is not detrimental to their health, raises questions of sovereignty and power over space, whether a state's territory, an individual's body, or a mandate of an international organization. Hence the central problem with the future of global health governance comes to be: how to force people, states, and communities to act in their own health interests whilst maintaining their own right to determine what their own interests are. This is the crux of what global health governance is about: contention over what is the right or best way of promoting better health outcomes, behavior, and the balance between multiple interests, actors, and knowledge.

Global health governance for whom?

Health governance has been globalized, securitized, medicalized, and criticized. The future research agenda will continue to focus on the need for innovations in responding collectively to emerging global threats quickly and effectively with minimal cost and maximum return. The current trend towards performance-oriented interventions, emphasizing social protection and joined-up health system strengthening requires new systems and scientific design that allows for rapid responses to new health issues, to speed up and streamline current approaches, and to introduce a technical element to the processes of global health governance that remove any multiplication of roles, competing systems, or lack of coordination. However, these innovations in science and technology need to be balanced against rights and responsibilities basic to any social contract between a state or intergovernmental organizations and citizens. Technological advancement and research to promote better global health outcomes must be measured against research that recognizes gender difference, human and civil rights, the long-term socio-economic impact of interventions, and wider issues of sovereignty of states and individual bodies, and the role of markets and militaries. Crucially, global health governance must not lose sight of the individuals it affects. Without such recognition we will see a shift to technocratic approaches to public health that do not consider people, the long-term policy implications, or the socio-economic drivers of ill-health. Striking the right balance between these dichotomies of global health governance will see greater moves forward in the provision of better health outcomes for all.

Notes

Foreword

1 For a discussion of this view, see Richard Dodgson and Kelley Lee, "Global Health Governance: A Conceptual Review," in Rorden Wilkinson and Steve Hughes, eds., *Global Governance: Critical Perspectives* (London: Routledge, 2002), 252–273; and Jeff Collin, Kelley Lee, and Karen Bissell, "Negotiating the Framework Convention on Tobacco Control: An Updated Politics of Global Health Governance," in *The Global Governance Reader*, ed. Rorden Wilkinson (London: Routledge, 2005), 92–110.

2 See Franklyn Lisk, *Global Institutions and the HIV/AIDS Epidemic* (London: Routledge, 2010); Kelley Lee, *The World Health Organization* (London: Routledge, 2009); David Hulme, *Global Poverty* (London: Routledge, 2010); Jennifer Clapp and Rorden Wilkinson, eds., *Global Governance, Poverty and Inequality* (London: Routledge, 2010); John Shaw, *Global Food and Agricultural Institutions* (London: Routledge, 2009); and James Vreeland, The International Monetary Fund (London: Routledge, 2007).

3 See Craig Murphy, *International Organization and Industrial Change: global governance since 1850* (Cambridge: Polity, 1994), especially Chapter 2.

4 www.transtanz.org.

Introduction

1 Mildred Blaxter, "What is Health?" in *Health and Disease: A Reader*, ed. Basiro Davey, Alastair Gray, and Clive Seale (Buckingham: Open University Press, 2004), 21–27.

2 Rene Dubos, "Mirage of Health," in *Health and Disease*, ed. Davey, Gray, and Seale, 4–9.

3 Walter Dowdle, "The Principles of Disease Elimination," *Bulletin of the WHO* 76, no. 2 supp (1998): 22–25.

4 Lise Wilkinson and Anne Hardy, *Prevention and Cure: the London School of Hygiene and Tropical Medicine: A Twentieth Century Quest for Global Public Health* (London: Kegan Paul, 2001), 30.

5 Ivan Illich, *Medical Nemesis: The Expropriation of Health* (New York: Pantheon Books, 1976).

6   Basiro Davey, Alastair Gray, and Clive Seale, "The Role of Medicine," in *Health and Disease*, ed. Davey, Gray, and Seale, 207–9.
7   Vicente Navarro, "The Mode of State Intervention in the Health Sector," in *Health and Disease*, ed. Davey, Gray, and Seale, 270–76.
8   Navarro, "The Mode of State Intervention in the Health Sector," 270–76.
9   Sandra Maclean and Sherri Brown, "Introduction: the Social Determinants of Global Health," in *Health for Some: the Political Economy of Global Health Governance*, ed. Sandra Maclean, Sherri Brown, and Pieter Fourie (Basingstoke: Palgrave Macmillan, 2009).
10   Kelley Lee, Suzanne Fustukian, and Kent Buse, "An Introduction to Global Health Policy," in *Health Policy in a Globalising World*, ed. Kelley Lee, Kent Buse, and Suzanne Fustukian (Cambridge: Cambridge University Press, 2002), 3–17.
11   Ronald Labonte and Renee Torgerson, "Interrogating Globalisation, Health and Development: Towards a Comprehensive Framework for Research, Policy and Political Action," in *Critical Perspectives in Public Health*, ed. Judith Green and Ronald Labonte (Abingdon: Routledge, 2008), 162–79.
12   Lee, Fustukian, and Buse, "An Introduction to Global Health Policy, 3–17."
13   Caroline Thomas and Martin Weber, "The Politics of Global Health Governance: Whatever Happened to 'Health for All By the Year 2000'?" *Global Governance* 10: 187–205.
14   Edward O'Neill, *Awakening Hippocrates* (Chicago: American Medical Association, 2006).
15   Jean Dreze and Amartya Sen, "Entitlement and Deprivation," in *Health and Disease*, ed. Davey, Gray, and Seale, 184–89.
16   Friedrich Engels, "Health: 1844," in *Health and Disease*, ed. Davey, Gray, and Seale, 141–46.
17   Victor Rodwin, "Health and Disease in Global Cities: a Neglected Dimension of National Health Policy," in *Networked Disease: Emerging Infections in the Global City*, ed. S. Harris Ali and Roger Keil (Chichester: Wiley-Blackwell, 2008), 27–48.
18   S. Harris Ali and Roger Keil, "Introduction: Networked Disease," in *Networked Disease*, ed. Ali and Keil, 1–12.
19   Ali and Keil, "Introduction: Networked Disease," 18.
20   O'Neill, *Awakening Hippocrates*; Thomas and Weber, "The Politics of Global Health Governance: Whatever Happened to 'Health for All By the Year 2000'?" 187–205; and Matthew Gandy, "Deadly Alliances: Death, Disease and the Global Politics of Public Health" in *Networked Disease*, ed. Ali and Keil, 172–85.
21   Kelley Lee and Richard Dodgson, "Globalization and Cholera: Implications for Global Governance," *Global Governance* 6, no. 2 (2000): 213–36.
22   Adrian Kay and Owain David Williams, "Introduction: the International Political Economy of Global Health Governance," in *Global Health Governance: Crisis, Institutions, and Political Economy*, ed. Adrian Kay and Owain David Williams (Basingstoke: Palgrave MacMillan, 2009), 1–23.
23   Kelley Lee, "Understandings of Global Health Governance: the Contested Landscape," in *Global Health Governance*, ed. Kay and Williams, 27–41.

24 Lee, "Understandings of Global Health Governance: the Contested Landscape," 27–41.
25 Maclean and Brown, "Introduction: the Social Determinants of Global Health."
26 Caroline Khoubesserion, "Global Health Initiatives: a Healthy Governance Response?" in *Innovation in Global Health Governance: Critical Cases*, ed. Andrew Cooper and John Kirton (Surrey: Ashgate, 2009), 285–306.

1 Approaches to global health governance

1 Daniel Tarantola, Andrew Byrnes, Michael Johnson, Lynn Kemp, Anthony Zwi, and Sofia Gruskin, *Human Rights, Health and Development*, University of New South Wales Technical Series Paper no. 08.1, 2008.
2 Villerme in Norman Daniels, Bruce Kennedy, and Ichiro Kawachi, "Health and Inequality, or, Why Justice is Good for our Health," in *Public Health, Ethics and Equity*, ed. Sudhir Anand, Fabienne Peter, and Amartya Sen (Oxford: Oxford University Press, 2004), 63–91.
3 Whitehead cited in Fabienne Peter, "Health Equity and Social Justice," in *Public Health, Ethics and Equity*, ed. Anand, Peter, and Sen, 93–106.
4 Amartya Sen, "Why Health Equity?" in *Public Health, Ethics and Equity*, ed. Anand, Peter, and Sen, 21–33.
5 Sudhir Anand, "Concern for Equity in Health," in *Public Health, Ethics and Equity* ed. Anand, Peter, and Sen, 15–20.
6 Fabienne Peter, "Health Equity and Social Justice."
7 Anand, "Concern for Equity in Health."
8 Inge Kaul, Isabelle Grunberg, and Marc Stern, "Defining Global Public Goods," in *Global Public Goods: International Cooperation in the 21st Century*, ed. Inge Kaul, Isabelle Grunberg, and Marc Stern (New York: Oxford University Press, 1999), 2–19; David Woodward and Richard Smith, "Global Public Goods and Health: Concepts and Issues," in *Global Public Goods for Health: Health Economic and Public Health Perspectives*, ed. Richard Smith, Robert Beaglehole, David Woodward, and Nick Drager (Oxford: Oxford University Press, 2003), 3–29.
9 Woodward and Smith, "Global Public Goods and Health: Concepts and Issues."
10 Lincoln Chen, Tim Evans, and Richard Cash, "Health as a Global Public Good," in *Global Public Goods*, ed. Kaul, Grunberg, and Stern, 284–304.
11 Kaul, Grunberg, Stern, "Defining Global Public Goods."
12 Kaul, Grunberg, Stern, "Defining Global Public Goods."
13 Woodward and Smith, "Global Public Goods and Health: Concepts and Issues."
14 Jayati Ghosh, "Medical knowledge" in *Global Public Goods for Health*, ed. Smith, Beaglehole, Woodward, and Drager, 119–36.
15 Ghosh, "Medical Knowledge."
16 Woodward and Smith, "Global Public Goods and Health: Concepts and Issues."
17 Gavin Mooney and Janet Dzator, "Global Public Goods for Health: a Flawed Paradigm?" in *Global Public Goods for Health*, ed. Smith, Beaglehole, Woodward, and Drager, 233–45.

18 Woodward and Smith, "Global Public Goods and Health: Concepts and Issues."

19 United Nations General Assembly, *The Right to Health: Note by the Secretary-General* (General assembly document A/63/263), 2008.

20 Mann in Paul Hunt, *Neglected Diseases: A Human Rights Analysis* (France: WHO Special Programme for Research and Training in Tropical Diseases).

21 Hunt, *Neglected Diseases: A Human Rights Analysis.*

22 Hunt, *Neglected Diseases: A Human Rights Analysis.*

23 Tarantola, Byrnes, Johnson, Kemp, Zwi, Gruskin, *Human Rights, Health and Development.*

24 *Ibid.*; Hunt, *Neglected Diseases: A Human Rights Analysis.*

25 Tarantola, Byrnes, Johnson, Kemp, Zwi, Gruskin, *Human Rights, Health and Development.*

26 Sources of European Right to Health law: European Social Charter (1961, revised, 1996); African Charter on Human and Peoples' rights (1981); Protocol to American Convention on Human Rights in the Area of Economic, Social and Cultural Rights "Protocol of San Salvador"; American Convention on Human Rights (1969); European Convention for the Promotion of Human Rights and Fundamental Freedoms (1950).

27 International Convention on the Elimination of All Forms of Racial Discrimination (CERD); Convention on the Elimination of All Forms of Discrimination Against Women (CEDAW) (articles 11 (1) *f*, 12 and 12 (2) (*b*); Convention on the Rights of the Child (CRC) (article 24); Convention on the Rights of Persons with Disabilities (article 25); and International Convention on the Protection of the Rights of All Migrant Workers and Members of their Families (articles 28, 43 9e, and 45 [c]).

28 For example, the International Conference on Primary Health Care (resulting in Alma Ata); and UN Millennium Development Goals, Declaration of Commitment on HIV/AIDS.

29 Helen Potts, "Accountability and the Right of Everyone to the Enjoyment of the Highest Attainable Standard of Physical and Mental Health," in *Governance of HIV/AIDS: Making Participation and Accountability Count*, ed. Sophie Harman and Franklyn Lisk (Abingdon: Routledge, 2009), 61–78.

30 Potts, "Accountability and the Right of Everyone to the Enjoyment of the Highest Attainable Standard of Physical and Mental Health."

31 Philippe Cullet, "Patents and Medicines: the Relationship between TRIPS and the Human Right to Health," *International Affairs* 79, no. 1 (2003): 139–60.

32 Sophie Harman, "The Causes, Contours and Consequences of the Multisectoral Response to HIV/AIDS," in *Governance of HIV/AIDS*, ed. Harman and Lisk, 165–79; and Sophie Harman, *The World Bank and HIV/AIDS: Setting a Global Agenda* (Abingdon: Routledge, 2010).

33 Joanna Santa Barbara and Graeme MacQueen, "Peace Through Health: Key Concepts," *The Lancet* 364 (2004): 384–86.

34 Barbara and MacQueen, "Peace Through Health: Key Concepts."

35 Colin McInnes, "National Security and Global Health Governance," in *Global Health Governance: Crisis, Institutions and Political Economy*, ed.

Adrian Kay and Owain David Williams (Basingstoke: Palgrave MacMillan, 2009).

36 P.W. Singer, "AIDS and International Security," *Survival* 44, no. 1 (2002): 145–58.

37 *Ibid.*

38 *Ibid.*

39 Colin McInnes, "HIV/AIDS and Security," *International Affairs* 82, no. 2 (2006): 315–26.

40 David Fidler and Lawrence Gostin, *Biosecurity in the Global Age: Biological Weapons, Public Health and the Rule of Law* (Stanford, CA: Stanford University Press, 2008).

41 Barry Kellman, *Bioviolence: Preventing Biological Terror and Crime* (Cambridge: Cambridge University Press, 2007).

42 Fidler and Gostin, *Biosecurity in the Global Age: Biological Weapons, Public Health and the Rule of Law.*

43 Kellman, *Bioviolence: Preventing Biological Terror and Crime.*

44 Fidler and Gostin, *Biosecurity in the Global Age: Biological Weapons, Public Health and the Rule of Law.*

45 *Ibid.*

46 The three bodies Kellman (2007) proposes are: 1. Commission on bioscience and security (committee); 2. Bioviolence prevention office (office); 3. Bioviolence committee on security council.

47 Ilona Kickbusch, "Global Health Governance: Some Theoretical Considerations on the New Political Space," in *Health Impacts of Globalization: Towards Global Governance*, ed. Kelley Lee (Basingstoke: Palgrave Macmillan, 2003), 192–203.

48 Colin McInnes and Kelley Lee, "Health, Security and Foreign Policy," *Review of International Studies* 32 (2006): 5–23.

49 Sandra Maclean, "Microbes, Mad Cows and Militaries: Exploring the Links Between Health and Security," *Security Dialogue* 39 (2008): 475–94.

50 McInnes and Lee, "Health, Security and Foreign Policy."

51 Stefan Elbe, "AIDS, Security, Biopolitics," *International Relations* 19, no. 4 (2005): 403–19.

52 McInnes, "National Security and Global Health Governance."

53 Elbe, "AIDS, Security, Biopolitics."

54 *Ibid.*

55 Michel Foucault, *The History of Sexuality: Volume I: An Introduction* (London: Penguin, 1976).

56 *Ibid.*, 141.

57 *Ibid.*, 155.

58 Elbe, "AIDS, Security, Biopolitics," 406.

59 Foucault, *The History of Sexuality: Volume I*, 126.

60 Elbe, "AIDS, Security, Biopolitics."

61 Foucault, *The History of Sexuality: Volume I*, 78.

62 *Ibid.*, 69.

63 Elbe, "AIDS, Security, Biopolitics," 413.

64 Foucault, *The History of Sexuality: Volume I*, 69.

65 *Ibid.*, 70.

66 Elbe, "AIDS, Security, Biopolitics."

67 Foucault, *The History of Sexuality: Volume I*, 157.

68 Stefan Elbe, "Risking Lives: AIDS, Security and Three Concepts of Risk," *Security Dialogue* 39, nos. 2–3 (2008).
69 Woody Caan and Dawn Hillier, "How Do We Perceive Risks?" in *Communicating Health Risks to the Public: a Global Perspective*, ed. Dawn Hillier (Aldershot: Gower Publishing Limited, 2006), 33–46; Dawn Hillier, *Communicating Health Risks to the Public: a Global Perspective* (Aldershot: Gower Publishing Limited, 2006).
70 WHO, *Risk Factors*, www.who.int/topics/risk_factors/en.
71 Claire Hooker, "SARS as a 'Health Scare'," in *Networked Disease: Emerging Infections in the Global City*, ed. S. Harris Ali and Roger Keil (Chichester: Wiley-Blackwell, 2008), 123–37.
72 Hooker, "SARS as a 'Health Scare'."
73 S. Harris Ali and Roger Keil, "Introduction: Networked Disease," in *Networked Disease: Emerging Infections in the Global City*, ed. S. Harris Ali and Roger Keil (Chichester: Wiley-Blackwell, 2008), 1–12.

2 Institutions of global health governance

1 Sophie Harman, "Fighting HIV and AIDS: Reconfiguring the State?" *Review of African Political Economy* 36, no. 121 (2009): 353–67.
2 Virginia Berridge, Kelly Loughlin, and Rachel Herring, "Historical Dimensions of Global Health Governance," in *Making Sense of Global Health Governance: A Policy Perspective*, ed. Kent Buse, Wolfgang Hein, and Nick Drager (Basingstoke: Palgrave Macmillan 2009), 28–46.
3 Berridge, Loughlin, Herring, "Historical Dimensions of Global Health Governance," 28–46.
4 Edward O'Neil, *Awakening Hippocrates* (Chicago: American Medical Association, 2006).
5 Lise Wilkinson and Anne Hardy, *Prevention and Cure: the London School of Hygiene and Tropical Medicine: a Twentieth Century Quest for Global Public Health* (London: Kegan Paul, 2001).
6 O'Neil, *Awakening Hippocrates*.
7 Berridge, Loughlin, Herring, "Historical Dimensions of Global Health Governance," 28–46.
8 Caroline Thomas and Martin Weber, "The Politics of Global Health Governance: Whatever Happened to 'Health for all by the year 2000'?" *Global Governance* 10 (2004): 187–205.
9 Berridge, Loughlin, Herring, "Historical Dimensions of Global Health Governance," 28–46; and Wilkinson and Hardy, *Prevention and Cure: the London School of Hygiene and Tropical Medicine: a Twentieth Century Quest for Global Public Health*, 28–46.
10 O'Neil, *Awakening Hippocrates*.
11 Marc A. Strassburg, "The Global Eradication of Smallpox," in *Health and Disease: A Reader*, ed. Basiro Davey, Alastair Gray, and Clive Seale (Buckingham: Open University Press), 259–63.
12 WHO, *About WHO* www.who.int/about/en.
13 Kelley Lee, *The World Health Organization* (London: Routledge, 2009).
14 WHO, *WHO Framework Convention on Tobacco Control* www.who.int/fctc/en.
15 Lee, *The World Health Organization*, 9.

16 John Kirton and Jenevieve Mannell, "The G8 and Global Health Governance," in *Governing Global Health: Challenge, Response, Innovation*, ed. Andrew Cooper, John Kirton, and Ted Schrecker (Aldershot: Ashgate, 2007), 115–46.

17 Lee, *The World Health Organization*, 100.

18 For further information on UNICEF see Richard Jolly, UNICEF (London: Routledge, forthcoming).

19 WHO-UNICEF, International Conference on Primary Healthcare (1979), and International Code of Marketing of Breastmilk Substitutes (1981).

20 UNFPA, "About UNFPA," www.unfpa.org/public/home/about.

21 UNFPA, "About UNFPA."

22 For further information on UNDP see Stephen Browne, *The United Nations Development Programme and System* (London: Routledge, 2011).

23 World Bank, World Bank Group Historical Chronology (2008), http://siteresources.worldbank.org/EXTARCHIVES/Resources/WB_Historical_Chronology_1944_2005.pdf.

24 Kent Buse, "Spotlight on International Organisations: the World Bank," *Health Policy and Planning* 9, no. 1 (1994): 95–99.

25 Buse, "Spotlight on International Organisations: the World Bank," 95–99.

26 Antonio Ugalde and Jeffrey Jackson, "The World Bank and International Health Policy: A Critical Review," *Journal of International Development* 7, no. 3 (1995): 525–41.

27 World Bank, *World Development Report: Investing in Health* (Washington, DC: World Bank, 1993).

28 Kent Buse and Catherine Gwin, "The World Bank and Global Cooperation in Health: The Case of Bangladesh," *The Lancet* 351 (1998): 665–69.

29 Kelley Lee and Hilary Goodman, "Global Policy Networks: The Propagation of Health Care Financing Reform Since the 1980s," in *Health Policy in a Globalising World*, ed. Kelley Lee, Suzanne Fustukian, and Kent Buse (Cambridge: Cambridge University Press, 2002), 97–119.

30 The World Bank underwent several reform processes under the presidency of James Wolfensohn (1995–2005). This reform saw the introduction of the bank's "good governance" agenda, and a shift away from structural adjustment towards the Comprehensive Development Framework approach that emphasized the role of governments, civil society, and sector-wide approaches to development projects. This period saw the bank reach out to its critics and involve itself in multiple development topics. Health and high-profile issues such as HIV/AIDS were a specific priority during this time.

31 Buse and Gwin, "The World Bank and Global Cooperation in Health: The Case of Bangladesh," 665–69.

32 Kamran Abbasi, "The World Bank and World Health: Changing Sides," *British Medical Journal* 318 (1999): 865–869; and Kamran Abbasi, "The World Bank and World Health: Under Fire," *British Medical Journal* 318 (1999): 1,003–6.

33 World Bank, *Healthy Development: The World Bank Strategy for Health, Nutrition and Population Results* (Washington, DC: World Bank, 2007).

34 Ross Buckley and Jonathan Baker, "IMF Policies and Health in Sub-Saharan Africa," in *Global Health Governance: Crisis, Institutions and Political Economy*, ed. Adrian Kay and Owain David Williams (Basingstoke: Palgrave MacMillan, 2009).

35 Gregg Bloche and Elizabeth Jungman, "Health policy and the World Trade Organisation," in *Globalization and Health*, ed. Ichiro Kawachi and Sarah Wamala (Oxford: Oxford University Press, 2007), 250–67.

36 Obijiofor Aginam, "Diplomatic Rhetoric or Rhetorical Diplomacy: the G8 and Global Health Governance," in *Governing Global Health: Challenge, Response, Innovation*, ed. Andrew Cooper, John Kirton, and Ted Schrecker (Aldershot: Ashgate, 2007), 147–55.

37 Aginam, "Diplomatic Rhetoric or Rhetorical Diplomacy: the G8 and Global Health Governance," 147–55.

38 Bloche and Jungman, "Health Policy and the World Trade Organisation," 250–67.

39 David Forsythe and Barbara Ann Rieffer-Flanagan, *The International Committee of the Red Cross* (London: Routledge, 2007).

40 ICRC, "Health," www.icrc.org/eng/what-we-do/health/index.jsp.

41 Interview with Peter Piot, executive director of UNAIDS 1995–2008, 6 July 2009, London.

42 Interview with Mario Raviglione, director of Stop TB Partnership, 31 August 2010, Geneva.

43 Anonymous interview, ICRC, 1 September 2010, Geneva.

44 Sophie Harman, *The World Bank and HIV/AIDS: Setting a Global Agenda* (London: Routledge, 2010).

45 Berridge, Loughlin, Herring, "Historical Dimensions of Global Health Governance."

46 *Ibid.*

47 Wilkinson and Hardy, *Prevention and Cure: the London School of Hygiene and Tropical Medicine: a Twentieth Century Quest for Global Public Health*, 67.

48 Wilkinson and Hardy, *Prevention and Cure: the London School of Hygiene and Tropical Medicine: a Twentieth Century Quest for Global Public Health*, 109.

49 Benjamin Page, "Evaluation and Accountability: with a Case Study of the Early Rockefeller Foundation," in *Philanthropic Foundations and the Globalization of Scientific Medicine and Public Health*, ed. Benjamin Page and David Valone (Plymouth: University Press of America, 2007).

50 Rockefeller in Joseph Kiger, *Philanthropists and Foundation Globalization* (London: Transaction Publishers, 2008), 33.

51 *Ibid.*

52 *Ibid.*

53 Rockefeller Foundation, "Global Health," www.rockefellerfoundation.org/who-we-are/our-focus/global-health.

54 Kiger, *Philanthropists and Foundation Globalization*, 33.

55 Rockefeller Foundation, "Global Health."

56 *Ibid.*

57 *Ibid.*

58 Interview with Laurie Lee, The Bill and Melinda Gates Foundation, 12 November 2010, London.

59 The Lancet editorial, "Bill Gates: a 21st Century Robin Hood?" *The Lancet* 365 (2005): 911–12.

60 Nirmala Ravishankar, Paul Gubbins, Rebecca Cooley, Katherine Leach-Kemon, Catherine Michaud, Dean Jamison, and Christopher Murray,

"Financing of Global Health: Tracking Development Assistance for Health from 1990 to 2007," *The Lancet* 373 (2009): 2,113–24; and David McCoy, Gayatri Kembhavi, Jinesh Patel, and Akish Luintel, "The Bill and Melinda Gates Foundation's Grant-Making Program for Global Health," The Lancet 373 (2009): 1,645–53.

61 Bill and Melinda Gates Foundation, "Global Health Program," www. gatesfoundation.org/global-health/Pages/overview.aspx.

62 Bill and Melinda Gates Foundation, "Global Health Program."

63 Gideon Rachman, "Inside the Gates Foundation," *Financial Times*, November 13/14 2010.

64 McCoy, Kembhavi, Patel, Luintel, "The Bill and Melinda Gates Foundation's Grant-Making Program for Global Health."

65 Interview with Laurie Lee.

66 Global Health Watch, *Global Health Watch 2: An Alternative World Health Report* (London: Zed Books, 2008).

67 *Ibid.*

68 *Ibid.*

69 Charles Piller, Edmund Sanders, and Robyn Dixon, "Dark Cloud Over Good Works of Gates Foundation," *Los Angeles Times*, January 2007.

70 The Lancet editorial, "Governance Questions at the Gates Foundation," *The Lancet* 369 (2007): 163.

71 Global Health Watch, *Global Health Watch 2: An Alternative World Health Report.*

72 Interview with Laurie Lee.

3 New actors in global health governance

1 Gill Walt, Neil Spicer, and Kent Buse, "Mapping the Global Health Architecture," in *Making Sense of Global Health Governance: a Policy Perspective*, ed. Kent Buse, Wolfgang Hein, and Nick Drager (Basingstoke: Palgrave Macmillan, 2009), 47–71.

2 John Kirton, Nickoei Roudev, Laura Sunderland, Catherine Kunz, and Jenilee Guebert, "Health Compliance in the G8 and APEC: the World Health Organisation's Role," in *Making Global Economic Governance Effective: Hard and Soft Law Institutions in a Crowded World*, ed. John Kirton, Marina Larionova, and Paulo Savona (Aldershot: Ashgate, 2010).

3 Kirton, Roudev, Sunderland, Kunz, and Guebert, "Health Compliance in the G8 and APEC: the World Health Organisation's Role."

4 John Kirton and Ella Kokotsis, "Keeping Faith with Africa's Health: Catalysing G8 Compliance," in *Governing Global Health: Challenge, Response, Innovation*, ed. Andrew Cooper, John Kirton, and Ted Schrecker (Aldershot: Ashgate, 2007), 157–79.

5 John Kirton and Jenevieve Mannell, "The G8 and Global Health Governance," in *Governing Global Health*, ed. Cooper, Kirton, and Schrecker, 115–46.

6 Kirton and Kokotsis, "Keeping Faith with Africa's Health: Catalysing G8 Compliance," 157–79.

7 Kirton and Mannell, "The G8 and Global Health Governance," 115–46; Obijifor Aginam, "Diplomatic Rhetoric or Rhetorical Diplomacy: the G8

and Global Health Governance," in *Governing Global Health*, ed. Cooper, Kirton, and Schrecker, 147–55.

8 Kirton and Mannell, "The G8 and Global Health Governance," 115–46.

9 Kirton, Roudev, Sunderland, Kunz, and Guebert, "Health Compliance in the G8 and APEC: the World Health Organisation's Role."

10 Ibid., 223.

11 Collenn O'Manique, "Global Health and Universal Human Rights: the Case for G8 Accountability," in *Governing Global Health*, ed. Cooper, Kirton, and Schrecker.

12 Ted Schrecker and Ronald Labonte, "What's Politics Got to do with it? Health, the G8, and the Global Economy," in *Globalization and Health*, ed. Ichiro Kawachi and Sarah Wamala (Oxford: Oxford University Press, 2007), 284–310.

13 Kirton and Mannell, "The G8 and Global Health Governance," 115–46.

14 Ted Schrecker, Ronald Labonte, and David Sanders, "Breaking Faith with Africa: the G8 and Population Health after Gleneagles," in *Governing Global Health*, ed. Cooper, Kirton, and Schrecker, 181–205; Ronald Labonte and Ted Schrecker, "Committed to Health for All? How the G7/8 Rate," *Social Science and Medicine* 59 (2004): 1,661–76; and Ronald Labonte, Ted Schrecker, David Sanders, and Wilma Meeus, *Fatal Indifference: The G8, Africa and Global Health* (Ottawa: University of Cape Town Press, 2004).

15 Labonte and Schrecker, "Committed to Health for All? How the G7/8 Rate," 1,661–76.

16 Kirton and Mannell, "The G8 and Global Health Governance," 115–46.

17 Global Fund, "Country Coordinating Mechanisms," www.theglobalfund. org/en/ccm/?lang=en.

18 Interview with Sandii Lwin, manager of the Bilateral and Multilateral Team Partnership Unit, Global Fund, 3 September 2010, Geneva.

19 Interview with Sandii Lwin.

20 Interview with Sandii Lwin.

21 Interview with Michael O'Connor, manager of the Civil Society Team, Global Fund, 3 September 2010, Geneva; interview with Cyrille Dubois, director of the West and Central Africa Unit, Global Fund, 2 September 2010, Geneva.

22 Interview Michael O'Connor; Interview David Winters, Director CCM Unit, Global Fund, 31 August 2010, Geneva, Switzerland.

23 Interview with Luca Occhini, vice director of the Latin America Caribbean Region, Global Fund, 31 August 2010, Geneva.

24 Interview with Cyrille Dubois.

25 Interview with Luca Occhini.

26 Global Fund, "Grant Portfolio," http://portfolio.theglobalfund.org/? lang=en; and "About the Global Fund," www.theglobalfund.org/en/ about/?lang=en.

27 Interview with Cyrille Dubois.

28 Interview with Cyrille Dubois.

29 Interview with Madeleine Leloup, senior advisor, Global Fund, 31 August 2010, Geneva.

30 Interview with Madeleine Leloup.

31 Interview with Cyrille Dubois.

32 Interview with Madeleine Leloup.

33 Interview with Anurita Bains, senior advisor, Global Fund, 3 September 2010, Geneva.

34 Darrin Grimsey and Mervyn Lewis, "The Governance of Contractual Relationships in Public-Private Partnerships," *Journal of Corporate Citizenship* 15 (2004): 91–109.

35 Joanna Chataway and James Smith, "The International AIDS Vaccine Initiative (IAVI): Is It Getting New Science and Technology to the World's Neglected Majority?" *World Development* 34, no. 1 (2006): 16–30.

36 Grimsey and Lewis, "The Governance of Contractual Relationships in Public-Private Partnerships," 91–109; and Chataway and Smith, "The International AIDS Vaccine Initiative (IAVI): Is It Getting New Science and Technology to the World's Neglected Majority?" 16–30.

37 Joanna Chataway, Stefano Brusoni, Eugenia Cacciatori, Rebecca Hanlin, and Luigi Orsenigo, "The International AIDS Vaccine Initiative (IAVI) in a Changing Landscape of Vaccine Development: a Public/Private Partnership as Knowledge Broker and Integrator," *European Journal of Development Research* 19 (2007): 100–17.

38 Kent Buse and Gill Walt, "Global Public-Private Partnerships: Part I – A New Development in Health?" *Bulletin of the World Health Organization* 78, no. 4 (2000): 549–61.

39 Chataway and Smith, "The International AIDS Vaccine Initiative (IAVI): Is It Getting New Science and Technology to the World's Neglected Majority?" 16–30.

40 Caroline Khoubesserion, "Global Health Initiatives: a Healthy Governance Response?" in *Innovation in Global Health Governance: Critical Cases*, ed. Andrew Cooper and John Kirton (Aldershot: Ashgate, 2009), 285–306.

41 Chataway, Brusoni, Cacciatori, Hanlin, and Orsenigo, "The International AIDS Vaccine Initiative (IAVI) in a Changing Landscape of Vaccine Development: a Public/Private Partnership as Knowledge Broker and Integrator," 100–17; and Chataway and Smith "The International AIDS Vaccine Initiative (IAVI): is it Getting New Science and Technology to the World's Neglected Majority?" 16–30.

42 Chataway, Brusoni, Cacciatori, Hanlin, and Orsenigo, "The International AIDS Vaccine Initiative (IAVI) in a Changing Landscape of Vaccine Development: a Public/Private Partnership as Knowledge Broker and Integrator," 100–17.

43 Chataway, Brusoni, Cacciatori, Hanlin, and Orsenigo, "The International AIDS Vaccine Initiative (IAVI) in a Changing Landscape of Vaccine Development: a Public/Private Partnership as Knowledge Broker and Integrator," 100–17; and Chataway and Smith, "The International AIDS Vaccine Initiative (IAVI): is it Getting New Science and Technology to the World's Neglected Majority?" 16–30.

44 IAVI, "Donors," www.iavi.org/about-IAVI/Pages/donors.aspx.

45 Chataway, Brusoni, Cacciatori, Hanlin, and Orsenigo, "The International AIDS Vaccine Initiative (IAVI) in a Changing Landscape of Vaccine Development: a Public/Private Partnership as Knowledge Broker and Integrator," 101.

46 GAVI, "Who we are," www.gavialliance.org/about/index.php.

47 "Innovation in Global Health: a Spoonful of Ingenuity," *The Economist*, 9 January 2010: 56–57.

48 "Innovation in Global Health: a Spoonful of Ingenuity," *The Economist.*
49 Kent Buse and Amalia Waxman, "Public-Private Health Partnerships: A Strategy for WHO," *Bulletin of the World Health Organization* 79, no. 8 (2001): 748–54.
50 "Innovation in Global Health: a Spoonful of Ingenuity," *The Economist.*
51 UNITAID, "Innovative Financing," www.unitaid.eu/en/about/innovative-financing-mainmenu-105/163.html.
52 "Innovation in Global Health: a Spoonful of Ingenuity," *The Economist.*
53 Andrew Cooper, *Celebrity Diplomacy* (Boulder: Paradigm Publishers, 2008).
54 John Street, "Celebrity Politicians: Popular Culture and Political Representation," *British Journal of Politics and International Relations* 6, no. 4 (2004): 435–52.
55 John Street, "Celebrity Politicians: Popular Culture and Political Representation," 435–52.
56 Examples of Goodwill Ambassadors: UNAIDS: Michael Ballack, Emmanuel Adebayor, Naomi Watts, HRH Princess Mathilde of Belgium, HRH Crown Princess Mette-Marit of Norway, and HSH Princess Stephanie of Monaco; WHO: Jet Li, Nancy Goodman Brinker, Liya Kebede, Yohei Sasakawa, Vienna Philharmonic Orchestra, Craig David (Stop TB Partnership), and Sylvie Vartan; Global Fund: Carla Bruni Sarkozy.
57 Andrew Cooper, *Celebrity Diplomacy.*
58 Jeremy Youde, "Ethical Consumerism or Reified Neoliberalism? Product (RED) and Private Funding for Public Goods," *New Political Science* 31, no. 2 (2009): 201–20.

4 The big three: malaria, HIV/AIDS, and tuberculosis

1 Randall Packard, *The Making of a Tropical Disease* (Baltimore: John Hopkins University Press, 2007).
2 WHO, *World Malaria Report* (Geneva: WHO, 2010), www.who.int/malaria/world_malaria_report_2010/en/index.html.
3 WHO, *World Malaria Report.*
4 A. J. Knell, *Malaria* (Oxford: Oxford University Press, 1991).
5 Packard, *The Making of a Tropical Disease.*
6 John Gallup and Jeffrey Sachs, "The Economic Burden of Malaria," *American Journal of Tropical Medicine* 64, nos. 1–2 (2001): 85–96.
7 Alexandria Shuler, *Malaria: Meeting the Global Challenge* (Boston: Gunn and Hain Publishers, 1985).
8 Knell, *Malaria.*
9 Shuler, *Malaria: Meeting the Global Challenge.*
10 R. Stephen Phillips, *Malaria* (London: Edward Arnold, 1983); and Packard, *The Making of a Tropical Disease.*
11 Knell, *Malaria.*
12 Mark Honigsbaum, *The Fever Trail: The Hunt for the Cure for Malaria* (Basingstoke: MacMillan, 2001).
13 Knell, *Malaria.*
14 *Ibid.*
15 *Ibid.*
16 Shuler, *Malaria.*

17 Walther Wernsdorfer, "The Importance of Malaria in the World," in *Malaria (Volume 1): Epidemiology, Chemotherapy, Morphology and Metabolism*, ed. Julius Kreier (London: Academic Press, 1980).

18 Shuler, *Malaria.*

19 Leo Slater, *War and Disease: Biomedical Research on Malaria in the Twentieth Century* (London: Rutgers University Press, 2009).

20 *Ibid.*

21 Wernsdorfer, "The Importance of Malaria in the World."

22 Phillips, *Malaria.*

23 Amy Staples, *The Birth of Development: How the World Bank, Foreign and Agriculture Office and World Health Organization Changed the World 1945–1965* (Kent, Ohio: The Kent State University Press, 2006).

24 Staples, *The Birth of Development.*

25 Knell, *Malaria.*

26 *Ibid.*; and Wernsdorfer, "The Importance of Malaria in the World."

27 "Is Malaria Eradication Possible?" *The Lancet* 370 (2007): 1,459.

28 Staples, *The Birth of Development.*

29 Penelope Key, "Malaria: Challenges for the 1990s," in *Malaria: Waiting for the Vaccine*, ed. Geoffrey Targett (Chichester: John Wiley and Sons, 1991), 1–4.

30 Shuler, *Malaria.*

31 Wernsdorfer, "The Importance of Malaria in the World."

32 Slater, *War and Disease.*

33 Knell, *Malaria.*

34 Bernhard Liese, "Malaria and the World Bank" in *Malaria*, ed. Targett, 7–9.

35 Ralph Henderson, "Malaria and the World Health Organisation," in *Malaria*, ed. Targett, 4–6.

36 Susan Foster, "The Distribution and Use of Antimalarial Drugs—Not a Pretty Picture," in *Malaria*, ed. Targett, 123.

37 Packard, *The Making of a Tropical Disease.*

38 Richard Feachem and Allison Phillips, "Malaria: 2 Years in the Fast Lane," *The Lancet* 373 (2009): 1,409–10.

39 Feachem and Phillips, "Malaria: 2 Years in the Fast Lane," 1,409.

40 "Reversing the Failures of Roll Back Malaria," *The Lancet* 365 (2005): 1,439.

41 Parliamentary Office of Science and Technology, *Tackling Malaria in Developing Countries*, Post Note No. 284, 2007.

42 Amir Attaran, Karen Barnes, Chris Curtis, Umberto d'Alessandro, Caterina Fanello, Mary Galinski, Gilbert Kokwaro, Sornchai Looareesuwan, Michael Makanga, Theonest Mutabingwa, Ambrose Talisuna, Jean Francois Trape, and William Watkins, "WHO, the Global Fund and Medical Malpractice in Malaria Treatment," *The Lancet* 363 (2004): 237–40.

43 Packard, *The Making of a Tropical Disease.*

44 Joel Bremen, Timothy Egan, and Gerald Keusch, "Introduction and Summary: The Intolerable Burden of Malaria," *American Journal of Tropical Medicine* 64, nos. 1–2 (2001).

45 Brian Greenwood, Kalifa Bajang, Christopher Whitty, and Geoffrey Targett, "Malaria," *The Lancet* 365 (2005): 1,487–98.

46 "Reversing the Failures of Roll Back Malaria."

47 In 2006, Attaran published an article in the prominent global health journal *The Lancet*, arguing that the World Bank had failed to live up to its financial commitment to malaria. The bank downsized the number of staff working on malaria from 7 in 1998 to 0 in 2002, and was unable to track or acknowledge how much of the $300–500 million it pledged to combat malaria it had spent. Instead of funding ACT efforts towards the treatment of malaria, in several instances the bank was seen to be recommending chloroquine. The World Bank defended these claims, suggesting that there was no evidence of false accounting or statistical manipulation in the Bank's work. However, the accusations against the Bank resemble a general problem within Roll Back Malaria and the governance of malaria and health more widely: the need for strong leadership; the distinction between money pledged and money spent; and the problem of sustaining short-term political will and the financing that accompanies it with long-term global health objectives.

48 Vassee Moorthy, Michael Good, and Adrian Hill, "Malaria Vaccine Developments," *The Lancet* 363 (2004): 150–56.

49 Hannah Kettler and Adrian Towse, *Public Private Partnerships for Research and Development: Medicines and Vaccines for Diseases of Poverty* (London: B SC Print Ltd, 2002).

50 Greenwood, Bajang, Whitty, and Targett, "Malaria."

51 UNAIDS, *Report on the Global AIDS Epidemic* (Geneva: UNAIDS, 2010), www.unaids.org/cn/media/unaids/contentassets/documents/unaidspublicati on/2010/20101123_globalreport_en.pdf.

52 Tony Barnett and Alan Whiteside, *AIDS in the Twenty-First Century: Disease and Globalization* (Basingstoke: Palgrave MacMillan, 2002).

53 Barnett and Whiteside, *AIDS in the Twenty-First Century: Disease and Globalization.*

54 *Ibid.*

55 Sophie Harman, *The World Bank and HIV/AIDS: Setting a Global Agenda* (London: Routledge, 2010).

56 Barnett and Whiteside, *AIDS in the Twenty-First Century: Disease and Globalization.*

57 *Ibid.*, 27.

58 Harman, *The World Bank and HIV/AIDS.*

59 Sophie Harman, "The Dual Feminization of HIV/AIDS," *Globalizations* 8, no. 2 (2011).

60 Harman, "The Dual Feminization of HIV/AIDS."

61 Virginia Berridge, *AIDS in the UK: the Making of Policy 1981–1994* (Oxford: Oxford University Press, 2002); Randy Shilts, *And the Bank Played On* (New York: St Martins Press, 1987); and Harman, *The World Bank and HIV/AIDS.*

62 Franklyn Lisk, *Global Institutions and the HIV/AIDS Crisis* (London: Routledge, 2010).

63 *Ibid.*

64 *Ibid.*

65 *Ibid.*

66 *Ibid.*

67 Harman, *The World Bank and HIV/AIDS.*

68 *Ibid.*

69 *Ibid.*
70 *Ibid.*
71 *Ibid.*
72 Stephen Morrison and Todd Summers, "United to Fight HIV/AIDS?" *Washington Quarterly* 26, no. 4 (2003): 177–93.
73 Morrison and Summers, "United to Fight HIV/AIDS?"
74 Harman, *The World Bank and HIV/AIDS.*
75 *Ibid.*
76 Chris Dye and Martien Borgdorff, "Global Epidemiology and Control of Tuberculosis," in *Handbook of Tuberculosis: Clinics, Diagnostics, Therapy and Epidemiology*, ed. S.H.E Kaufmann and P. van Helden (London: Wiley-VCH, 2008).
77 Carol Dyer, *Tuberculosis* (Oxford: Greenwood, 2010).
78 *Ibid.*
79 WHO, "Tuberculosis," www.who.int/topics/tuberculosis/en.
80 Dyer, *Tuberculosis.*
81 Dye and Borgdorff, "Global Epidemiology and Control of Tuberculosis."
82 WHO, "Tuberculosis."
83 Dye and Borgdorff, "Global Epidemiology and Control of Tuberculosis."
84 *Ibid.*
85 Dyer, *Tuberculosis.*
86 Felissa Cohen and Jerry Durham, *Tuberculosis: a Sourcebook for Nursing Practice* (New York: Springer Publishing Company, 1995).
87 WHO, "Tuberculosis."
88 Dyer, *Tuberculosis*; J.N. Hays, *The Burdens of Disease: Epidemics and Human Response in Western History—Revised Edition* (London: Rutgers University Press, 2009); and Selman Waksman, *The Conquest of Tuberculosis* (London: Robert Hale Ltd, 1964).
89 Hays, *The Burdens of Disease: Epidemics and Human Response in Western History—Revised Edition.*
90 Anonymous (an English physician), *Tuberculosis: Its Treatment and Cure with the Help of Umckaloabo (Stevens)* (London: B. Fraser and Co., 1931).
91 George Bankoff, *The Conquest of Tuberculosis* (London: McDonald and Co., 1946); Sigard Knopf, *Tuberculosis: as a Disease of the Masses and How to Combat It* (New York: Arno Press, 1977); and George Meachen, *A Short History of Tuberculosis* (London: John Bale, Sons and Danielsson Ltd, 1936).
92 Frances Smith, *The Retreat of Human Tuberculosis 1850–1950* (London: Croom Helm, 1988); Hays, *The Burdens of Disease: Epidemics and Human Response in Western History—Revised Edition.*
93 Robert Lovell, *Taking the Cure: the Patient's Approach to Tuberculosis* (New York: The Macmillan Company, 1948).
94 *Ibid.*
95 Smith, *The Retreat of Human Tuberculosis 1850–1950.*
96 *Ibid.*
97 Hays, *The Burdens of Disease: Epidemics and Human Response in Western History—Revised Edition*; and Dyer, *Tuberculosis.*
98 *Ibid.*
99 During this time anti-tuberculosis initiatives were established in: Argentina, Australia, Austria, Belgium, Canada, Czechoslovakia, Denmark, Egypt, Finland, France, Germany, Holland, Hungary, India, Ireland, Italy,

Japan, New Zealand, Norway, Poland, Portugal, Rumania, South Africa, Spain, Sweden, Switzerland, the USA and the USSR.
100 Hays, *The Burdens of Disease: Epidemics and Human Response in Western History—Revised Edition*; Dyer, *Tuberculosis.*
101 Smith, *The Retreat of Human Tuberculosis 1850–1950*; and Hays, *The Burdens of Disease.*
102 *Ibid.*
103 Dyer, *Tuberculosis.*
104 Dye and Borgdorff, "Global Epidemiology and Control of Tuberculosis."
105 Gill Walt, "The Politics of Tuberculosis: the Role of Process and Power," in *Tuberculosis: an Interdisciplinary Perspective*, ed. John Porter and John Grange (London: Imperial College Press, 1999), 67–98.
106 Smith, *The Retreat of Human Tuberculosis 1850–1950.*
107 R.G. Hewinson, "Tuberculosis Vaccines for the World," *Tuberculosis: special issue TB Vaccines for the World* 85, nos. 1–2 (2005): 1–6; and Michael Brennan, "The Tuberculosis Vaccine Challenge," *Tuberculosis: special issue TB Vaccines for the World* 85, 1–2 (2005): 7–12.
108 Paul Shears, *Tuberculosis Control Programmes in Developing Countries* (Oxford: Oxfam Practical Health Guide No. 4, 1988).
109 Waksman, *The Conquest of Tuberculosis.*
110 Lee Reichman, *Timebomb: the Global Epidemic of Multi-Drug Resistant Tuberculosis* (London: McGraw Hill, 2002).
111 Walt, "The Politics of Tuberculosis: the Role of Process and Power."
112 Among these pioneers are Christopher Bennet (1617–55); Thomas Willis (1621–75); Thomas Sydenham (1624–89); William Stark (1741–70); James Carson (1772–1843); George Boddington (1799–1882); William Budd (1811–80); Leopold Auenbrugger (1722–1809); Jean Nicholas Corvisart (1755–1820); Gaspard Laurent Bayle (1774–1816); Rene Theophile Hyacinthe Laennec (1781–1826); Pierre Adolphe Piorry (1794–1892); Jean-Antoine Villemin (1827–92); Edward Livingstone Trudeau (1848–1915); and Robert Koch (1843–1910).
113 Reichman, *Timebomb: the Global Epidemic of Multi-Drug Resistant Tuberculosis.*
114 Gary Maartens and Robert Wilkinson, "Tuberculosis," *The Lancet* 370 (2007): 2,030–2,043.
115 Dyer, *Tuberculosis.*
116 *Ibid.*
117 Janet Cornwall, "Tuberculosis: a Clinical Problem of International Importance," *The Lancet* 349 (1997): 660–61.
118 Lee Reichman, "How to Ensure the Continued Resurgence of Tuberculosis," *The Lancet* 347 (1996): 175–77.
119 Walt, "The Politics of Tuberculosis: the Role of Process and Power."
120 Shears, *Tuberculosis Control Programmes in Developing Countries.*
121 *Ibid.*
122 Dyer, *Tuberculosis*; and John Grange, "The Global Burden of Tuberculosis," in *Tuberculosis: an Interdisciplinary Perspective*, ed. John Porter and John Grange (London: Imperial College Press, 1999), 3–31.
123 Walt, "The Politics of Tuberculosis: the Role of Process and Power."
124 WHO, *Treatment of Tuberculosis: Guidelines for National Programmes* (Geneva: WHO, 1993).

125 Dyer, *Tuberculosis.*
126 Dermot Maher and Mario Raviglione, "Global Epidemiology of Tuberculosis," *Clinics in Chest Medicine: Tuberculosis* 26, no. 2 (2005): 167–82.
127 Maartens and Wilkinson, "Tuberculosis."128
    WHO, *Treatment of Tuberculosis: Guidelines for National Programmes.*
129 Maartens and Wilkinson, "Tuberculosis."
130 G. Bloomfield, *Tuberculosis: Trends and Opportunities* (London: PJB Publications Ltd, 1995).
131 Maher and Raviglione, "Global Epidemiology of Tuberculosis."
132 Dye and Borgdorff, "Global Epidemiology and Control of Tuberculosis."
133 *Ibid.*
134 Maartens and Wilkinson, "Tuberculosis."
135 WHO/IUATLD, *Anti-Tuberculosis Drug Resistance in the World—3rd Global Report* (Geneva: WHO, 2004).
136 DFID, Health and Population Division, "A Donor's Perspective on Tuberculosis in International Health," *The Lancet* 353 (1999): 1,006.
137 David Wilkinson, "Managing Tuberculosis Case-Loads in African Countries," *The Lancet* 349 (1997): 882.
138 Maher and Raviglione, "Global Epidemiology of Tuberculosis."
139 Dye and Borgdorff, "Global Epidemiology and Control of Tuberculosis."
140 Virginia Gleissberg, "The Threat of Multidrug Resistance: Is Tuberculosis Ever Untreatable or Uncontrollable?" *The Lancet* 353 (1999): 998–99; and Maher and Raviglione, "Global Epidemiology of Tuberculosis."
141 Maher and Raviglione, "Global Epidemiology of Tuberculosis."
142 WHO, *Implementing the WHO Stop TB Strategy: a Handbook for National Tuberculosis Control Programmes* (Geneva: WHO, 2008).
143 Donald Enarson, Hans Rieder, and Thuridur Arnadottir, *Tuberculosis Guide for Low Income Countries (International Union Against Tuberculosis and Lung Disease)* (Frankfurt: pmi Verlagsgruppe, 1994); and Donald Enarson, Hans Rieder, Thuridur Arnadottir, and Arnaud Trebucq, *Management of Tuberculosis: A Guide for Low Income Countries (International Union Against Tuberculosis and Lung Disease)* (Aachen: Miseror, 2000).
144 Klaus Jochem and John Walley, "Tuberculosis in High-Prevalence Countries: Current Control Strategies and their Technical and Operational Limitations," in *Tuberculosis: An Interdisciplinary Perspective*, ed. John Porter and John Grange (London: Imperial College Press, 1999), 123–65.
145 Jochem and Walley, "Tuberculosis in High-Prevalence Countries: Current Control Strategies and their Technical and Operational Limitations."
146 Gleissberg, "The Threat of Multidrug Resistance: Is Tuberculosis Ever Untreatable or Uncontrollable?"
147 John Grange, "The Global Burden of Tuberculosis," 24–25.
148 Bloomfield, *Tuberculosis: Trends and Opportunities.*
149 Richard Coker, *Migration, Public Health and Compulsory Screening for TB and HIV* (London: IPPR Asylum and Migration Working Paper 1, 2003).
150 Gleissberg, "The Threat of Multidrug Resistance: Is Tuberculosis Ever Untreatable or Uncontrollable?" 998.
151 Lee Reichman, *Timebomb: the Global Epidemic of Multi-drug Resistant Tuberculosis.*
152 WHO/IUATLD, *Anti-tuberculosis Drug Resistance in the World—3rd Global Report.*

5 Neglected health

1 WHO, *Global Plan to Combat Neglected Diseases 2008–2015*, (Geneva: WHO, 2008): http://whqlibdoc.who.int/hq/2007/WHO_CDS_NTD_2007.3_ eng.pdf.
2 *Ibid.*
3 *Ibid.*
4 Marc Strassburg, "The Global Eradication of Smallpox," in *Health and Disease: A Reader*, ed. Basiro Davey, Alastair Gray and Clive Seale (Buckingham: Open University Press, 2004), 259–63.
5 World Bank, *World Bank Group Historical Chronology*, 2008: http://siteresources.worldbank.org/EXTARCHIVES/Resources/WB_Historical_ C hronology_1944_2005.pdf.
6 *Ibid.*, 148.
7 WHO, *Gender, Women and Health*: www.who.int/gender/en.
8 WHO, *Strategy for Integrating Gender Analysis and Actions into the Work of WHO: WHO Gender Strategy* (Geneva: WHO, 2009): www. who.int/gender/documents/gender/9789241597708/en/index.html.
9 UNFPA, *Gender Equality: a Cornerstone of Development*: www.unfpa. org/gender.
10 World Bank, *Better Health for Women and Families: The World Bank's Reproductive Health Action Plan 2010–2015* (Washington, DC: World Bank, 2010): http://siteresources.worldbank.org/INTPRH/Resources/ 376374–1261312056980/RHAP_Pub_8–23–10web.pdf.
11 UN, *Reduce Child Mortality Factsheet*: www.un.org/millenniumgoals/pdf/ MDG_FS_4_EN.pdf.
12 World Bank, *Better Health for Women and Families: The World Bank's Reproductive Health Action Plan.*
13 WHO, *Consensus for Maternal, Newborn and Child Health* (Geneva: WHO, 2009): www.who.int/pmnch/topics/maternal/consensus_12_09.pdf.
14 WHO, *Consensus for Maternal, Newborn and Child Health.*
15 WHO, *Consensus for Maternal, Newborn and Child Health.*
16 WHO, "Making Pregnancy Safer: New WHO Department of Maternal, Child and Adolescent Health to be Created," www.who.int/making_ pregnancy_safer/new_mch/en/index.html.
17 UNFPA, "Safe Motherhood," www.unfpa.org/public/home/mothers.
18 *Ibid.*
19 UNICEF, "Healthy Women, Better World," www.unicef.org/maternalhea lth/index_587.htm.
20 World Bank, *Better Health for Women and Families: The World Bank's Reproductive Health Action Plan 2010–2015.*
21 *Ibid.*
22 UNIFEM, "About Us," www.unifem.org.

Select bibliography

The field of global health governance is rapidly expanding with new books and research regularly being published. The books listed here are introductory texts for further reading on the subject. In addition to the books listed, periodicals such as *The Lancet* and *Social Science and Medicine* are a good source of new research and opinion pieces on emerging global health issues.

S. Anand, F. Peter, and A. Sen, eds., *Public Health, Ethics and Equity* (Oxford: Oxford University Press, 2006) provides a good introduction to understandings of public health, justice, and equality for both those new to health or ethics and political philosophy.

Tony Barnett and Alan Whiteside, *AIDS in the Twenty-First Century* (London: Palgrave MacMillan, 2006) is a comprehensive account of HIV and AIDS as exceptional health issues and the politics and machinations of the epidemic and its response.

Andrew Cooper, John Kirton, and Ted Schrecker, eds., *Governing Global Health: Challenge, Response, Innovation* (Aldershot: Ashgate, 2007) is one of the first books in the Ashgate series on global health governance; helpful for its specific focus on the G8 and the health Millennium Development Goals.

Global Health Watch, *Global Health Watch 2* (London: Zed Books, 2008) is a critical assessment of various actors and issues within global health. Punchy, case-study-based assessment of current frameworks of global health governance as a basis for alternatives. A good source of updated information, check for the most recent reports.

Judith Green and Ronald Labonté, *Critical Perspectives in Public Health* (London: Routledge, 2007) extends common themes of health and globalization to relate to specific health issues and spaces of public health often neglected in comparable books.

Ivan Illich, *Medical Nemesis: The Expropriation of Health* (New York: Pantheon Books, 1976) is a critical account of the medicalization of society and medicine in general. Interesting cross-reference to research on the securitization of health.

Adrian Kay and Owain Williams, eds., *Global Health Governance: Crisis, Institutions and Political Economy* (London: Palgrave MacMillan, 2009) contains interesting chapters focusing on international political economy of health through focus on financial institutions and issues of globalization and disease.

Kelley Lee, *The World Health Organization (WHO)* (London: Routledge, 2009) is the definitive book on the WHO written by one of the global experts on the institution.

Kelley Lee, Kent Buse, and Suzanne Fustukian, *Health Policy in a Globalising World* (Cambridge: Cambridge University Press, 2002) is a comprehensive edited volume on the relationship between globalization and health and the frameworks and arrangements that support this.

Sandra J. Maclean, Sherri Brown, and Pieter P. Fourie, eds., *Health for Some: The Political Economy of Global Health Governance* (Basingstoke: Palgrave Macmillan, 2009) is an excellent introduction to central themes and actors within global health governance. Extends beyond well-documented security and globalization approaches to health to be much more comprehensive in scope and concise in understanding.

Richard Smith, Robert Beaglehole, David Woodward, and Nick Drager, eds., *Global Public Goods for Health: Health Economic and Public Health Perspectives* (Oxford: Oxford University Press, 2003) is a comprehensive and thorough understanding of public goods for health and health as a public good. Goes beyond basic introductions to relate to case studies.

Index

132; Health 4+ 131; HIV/AIDS
101–2; maternal/child health 128,
129–33; MDGs 122, 128, 129,
130, 131, 132; neglected 10, 11,
15, 122, 128–34, 137; related to
gender-specific roles 133–34;
UNFPA 129, 131–32; UNIFEM/
UN Women 132–33; WHO's
Gender, Women and Health
Network 128, 129; World Bank
129, 132, 133; *see also* neglected
disease/health

World Bank 1, 6, 10, 28, 45, 46–50;
community engagement 48, 49;
criticism 47; Feachem, Richard
48; financing of health sector
programs 46–47, 48–49, 50; G8/
G20 69, 70; Gates Foundation 62;
Global Fund 72; "good
governance" agenda 48, 49, 152;
health as a global public good 48;
health/poverty/development
relationship 46; health system
strengthening 127, 132, 134, 137;
HIV/AIDS 105–6, 118–19
(Multi-Country AIDS Program

106); malaria 96, 97, 158;
maternal health 19, 89;
McNamara, Robert 46, 127;
multisectoralism/SWAps 18, 19,
47, 48–49, 106, 152; neglected
tropical disease 126–27; NGOs 56;
origins 46; PPPs 77; privatization
47; reduction of state provision of
health 47; reform processes 47,
152; structural adjustment/
neoliberal reform 47, 48, 49, 152;
tuberculosis 116, 119; WHO 10,
39, 48, 65; Wolfensohn, James
152; women's health 129, 132, 133

WTO (World Trade Organization) 6,
10, 28, 48, 50, 51–54; FCTC
53–54; GATT (General
Agreement on Tariffs and Trade)
51; health of working populations
51–52; health provision 53;
migration 51, 52; right to health
53; role 51, 53, 54; trade/global
health relationship 51; trade
liberalization and health concerns
51, 53–54; WHO 10, 54; *see also*
trade; TRIPs